Curiosities Series

IOWA
Curiosities

Quirky Characters,
Roadside Oddities & Other
Offbeat Stuff

Dan Coffey and Eric Jones
with Berit Thorkelson

The
Globe
Pequot
Press

GUILFORD, CONNECTICUT

The information in this book was confirmed at press time. We recommend, however, that you call establishments to obtain current information before traveling.

Photos by the authors unless otherwise noted.
Cover photos: top, Catherine Cole; center, Berit Thorkelson
Text design by Bill Brown
Layout by Debbie Nicholias
Maps by XNR Productions, Inc. © The Globe Pequot Press

ISSN 1551-7985
ISBN 0-7627-2548-6

Manufactured in the United States of America
First Edition/First Printing

ACKNOWLEDGMENTS

Thanks to all those Iowans, from Sioux City to Muscatine and everywhere in between, who invited us into their homes, told us their stories, showed us collections, gave us impromptu history lessons, even fed us, and made a couple of characters, quirky in their own right, feel at home. We are additionally grateful to Berit Thorkelson, our intrepid guide to some of western Iowa's most curious attractions, including the world's largest Cheeto, displayed on its own hand-blown glass pedestal. And finally our thanks to Mary Norris and Gillian Belnap of The Globe Pequot Press for their support and unflagging patience.

Contents

INTRODUCTION

O ddity is in the eye of the beholder.

I traveled out east this summer in a 1997 Geo Prizm with Johnson County, Iowa plates. Not long after crossing the border into New Hampshire on Interstate 95, I noticed what appeared to be a father and son on a motorcycle pulling up alongside us to pass. Even though I was paying close attention to the road ahead, my hands at ten and two o'clock on the wheel, knuckles just the slightest bit pale (east coast driving can be a little more demanding than corn belt driving), I couldn't help but notice that the pair was passing us very, very slowly. What's more, I had that uncanny but unmistakable feeling that I was being watched. Sure enough, when I looked to my left, both pop and progeny were staring at us from behind the visors of their helmets with a wide-eyed curiosity that made me feel a bit like an exhibit at the zoo. "I saw them staring at us from way back," my companion told me. "I think they were looking at our Iowa plates."

And so it was that simply by driving 1,127 miles east my companion and I, our small black sedan, and its license plate with the gray outline of a farmyard beneath the vague silhouette of a city skyline and a patch of baby blue sky had become Iowa curiosities. "I hope you got a good close look, son," I imagined the father saying at their next rest stop. "That couple in the Geo, they were from Ohio." And I imagined the son looking up at his father, his guide to this big, strange world, and asking, "Isn't that where they grow all those potatoes?"

If you've spent much time on either coast, then you know that for most Americans Iowa is more of a hazy idea than a reality, more symbol than actual state. When it's not confused with Idaho or Ohio, two other states with what my Connecticut friend likes to call "skewed vowel-to-consonant ratios," Iowa means small towns, farms, corn, covered bridges, and not a whole lot else. In fact, it seems to come as a bit of a shock to coastal denizens that people, real people, actually live here. "Iowa?" the Californian will bellow incredulously when he meets you, as if Iowa is another Timbuktu. "Who lives in Iowa?" Or worse, a New Yorker might ask you in earnest, "Why do you live in *Iowa*?" with more than a hint of pity in her voice, as if settling in West Des Moines were akin to living on a Russian space station that's having technical problems with its life support systems.

I'm not complaining, though, at least not too loudly. After all, one of the main reasons Midwesterners travel in the first place is to be strangers for a while, to make our ordinary selves a little more exotic than we have a right to be, and then pleasantly or not so pleasantly bump up against the ways we're misunderstood. Being an Iowan in New York City or in Paris feels different than being an Iowan in Cedar Rapids, and it's partly that unfamiliar way of being ourselves that we travelers seek out.

Mostly, though, we hit the road in search of the new, the strange, and the extraordinary in this great big world. We leave home to discover something our neighbors haven't ever seen before, take pictures of it, and bring the evidence back home for show and tell. We head out to be impressed. And although some people think you need to cross whole continents and wide blue seas to see things you've never seen, or never even imagined seeing before, while researching this book we discovered that oddity is a lot closer to home than you might think, sometimes even unsettlingly so.

So what curiosities did we find in our own back yard? How about a life-size concrete pink elephant wearing a top hat? Or a Guinness-certified world's largest collection of salt and pepper shakers (more than 14,000, and counting)? And what about a man who turns a grain silo into a three-story house, or a contest where the players throw cast iron skillets at scarecrows, or a museum devoted to the humble lawnmower, or a Trappist Monastery where the monks build coffins for their daily bread? In the next county over, maybe even just across town, down a dirt road you've never taken, you'll find all the oddity you're looking for and more, at a fraction of the cost of a ticket to Bora Bora.

So here's to quirkiness close at hand. Here's to all the ways we can be surprised by what we thought we knew just by driving a little farther and taking a closer look. Seeking out the unfamiliar isn't for the fainthearted. It takes courage to leave the couch and say hello to a stranger, particularly a stranger who's on the strange side. And the world's biggest anything can be scary, even if it's something as seemingly harmless as an overpuffed Cheeto. Dear readers, fellow travelers, soon-to-be strangers, we know you're up to the challenge. Enjoy.

—Eric Jones

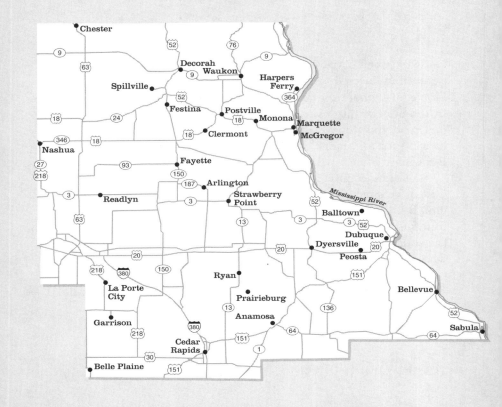

NORTHEAST

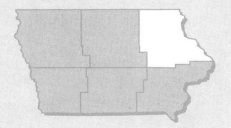

NORTHEAST

P LAY P RISONER FOR A D AY R IGHT
B ESIDE 1 , 2 0 0 I NMATES
A n a m o s a

I owa's own version of Alcatraz is the Anamosa State Penitentiary, a maximum-security facility housing more than 1,200 inmates. Built in 1872 from local limestone, the prison is an architectural manifestation of deep depression: Fortress-style stone walls the color of overcast sky rise up, and up, and up, high enough to contain four tiers of barred cells, one on top of another, in open cell blocks as long as football fields. As tantalizing a place as it sounds, you can't tour the penitentiary building without either a good reason or a heavy debt to society, but you can visit the Anamosa State Penitentiary Museum to get a taste of life in Anamosa's big house over the past century and a half.

Located beside the penitentiary in a converted outbuilding that once housed a cheese factory, the Anamosa Museum is a small treasure trove of information about the prison's construction, famous and not-so-famous inmates, guards, and prison life. One highlight is a replica of an old prison cell: Step inside, slam the door, and try not to scream when someone says "life sentence." Truth be told, the real penitentiary with its living,

A big house with surprisingly cramped rooms.

breathing inmates may be a bit too close for comfort to take much pleasure in playing convict—a sign alongside the prison driveway even asks visitors to lock their car doors before they enter so that escaping inmates can't make an easy getaway.

The museum has archived loads of information about some less-than-savory characters, including Wesley Elkins, an eleven-year-old boy who served a life sentence at Anamosa for murdering his parents in 1889, first shooting his father in his bed and then, unable to find wadding to reload the rifle, bludgeoning his stepmother to death with a club. And do you remember John Gacy, one of America's most notorious serial killers in U.S. history? Convicted in 1980 of murdering thirty-three young men, Gacy spent two years at the penitentiary in the sixties and was reportedly a model prisoner.

It may not be the most cheery weekend activity, but a visit to Anamosa's prison museum will delight crime and punishment fans and history buffs alike. Just be sure to check the back seat before you leave the parking lot.

5,300 *H A T S* (*A N D* *C O U N T I N G*) *A N D* *A* *M O N E Y* *P I T*
Arlington

The Castle House is a fitting name for the Queen Anne–style structure in tiny Arlington that contains Faith Mitchell's extraordinary collection of hats, not only because it vaguely resembles a castle, with its weathered clapboard turret, but because it is, for all intents and purposes, a ruin. To say the paint is peeling would be inaccurate; it has already peeled, and weathered gray (and still weathering) has become the Castle House's new color. The small front porch tilts away from the house just slightly, and the boards moan when you walk on them to let you know their age. Up the creaky stairs and to the left you'll see hats, hats, and more hats, adorned with every imaginable feather, ribbon, and ornamental flower, but you'll also see right through the old plaster walls to the lathing and horsehair underneath.

The Castle House Preservation Society, or CHPS, a local nonprofit organization dedicated to restoring the Castle House and securing a permanent home for the more than 5,300 hats in the collection, has made some improvements to the building over the last decade, including replastering the kitchen and replacing the second-story porch, but the house decidedly remains, in polite real estate terms, a real fixer-upper. And repairs continue. When I asked Barbara Schuchmann, primary hat indexer of the collection and one of the two main tour guides, about recent renovations, she told me matter-of-factly, "We just made $45 in repairs this month." (Needless to say, renovation progress doesn't proceed quite as quickly for the Castle House as it does for, say, the featured home on *This Old House*.)

Faith Mitchell, a local farm wife, began collecting hats decades ago and over the years acquired enough caps, bonnets, and hats from places as far-flung as Spain, Germany, and China to fill a . . . well, to fill a castle house. In 1987 she and her family, owners of Mitchell's House of Hats, donated her vast collection to CHPS, and the hats and the Castle House have been a pair ever since. A more perfect setting for the collection is hard to imagine. All those old-fashioned hats tucked away in such a humble setting make you feel as if you're rummaging around in your grandmother's ramshackle attic, discovering treasures she saved just for you.

The sheer variety of hats, in an era dominated by baseball caps plastered with sports-team mascots and corporate logos, is astounding. Bertha, whose number is listed below, and a few other CHPS volunteers indexed and affixed labels to a good many of the hats, which range from simple bonnets and classic top hats from the late nineteenth century to wild, flowery affairs that would have done any 1920s Chicago flapper proud. Racks and racks of hats fill the dark bedrooms, the living room, and the hallways with manufacturers and designers including Christian Dior, Alice May of Fifth Avenue, and Montgomery Ward. The collection also includes more than 1,700 accessories—including gloves, scarves, handkerchiefs and other sartorial garnishes—that seem, for the most part, the forgotten castoffs of a dressed-down America. It's hard to resist jumping right into the pile and playing dress up.

People keep donating hats to the collection, so if you're looking for baseball caps, you'll find some of those, too, in the far bedroom, as well as a cap affixed with a beer-can holder at each temple and two curled straws intended for the hat-owner's mouth. But, surely, this was a recent addition; judging from the bulk of the collection, Faith Mitchell had far more refined tastes in headwear. Further validation of her taste is that she chose a perfect place to hang all her 5,300 hats. Donations to help repair the plaster are appreciated—really appreciated.

Castle House has no heat or electricity, so it's advisable to visit during the warmer months. Before you go be sure to call either Bertha Schuchmann at (563) 633–3385 or Alice Miller at (563) 633–5492 to make an appointment. (Both serve as tour guides, and both knew Faith Mitchell personally.) Arlington is located on Highway 187, about 5 miles north of Highway 3. Heading north into town, take a right at the library and go about a block and a half. The Castle House will be the Munster-family-mansion-style fixer-upper on the left.

WHERE DINERS OUTNUMBER ALL THE LOCALS 4 TO 1
Balltown

*F*ood-savvy travelers know a good test of any wayside restaurant is whether or not the locals eat there. See only out-of-county and out-of-state plates in the lot, and you may want to keep hunting for native diners, unless, of course, you happen to be in a place like Balltown, located north of Dubuque on the Mississippi's Great River Road, where locals are a bit of an endangered species. Balltown, perched on a bluff high above the Mississippi offering truly spectacular views of the river valley below, has a population listed at approximately sixty-four people, or twenty families, about the size of your average high-school football team. Even if half the town dined out for every meal, they wouldn't be so easy to track down.

Not to fear. There's only one restaurant in Balltown, and the food there is very good. Breitbach's, which lays claim to the title of oldest bar and restaurant in Iowa, has seating for four

times Balltown's population; on the busiest days owner Mike
Breitbach says, "We can serve more than thirteen, fourteen
hundred people." And trying to find the locals in a crowd like
that is a whole lot harder than finding Waldo.

Besides the delicious, made-from-scratch food, Breitbach's is
a living museum, filled with antiques, old photographs, and
other memorabilia. Century-old rifles and pistols, their polished
wood stocks shimmering in the light, hang above the bar; old
farm implements, tools, and lots of old lanterns dangle from
the rafters; handmade quilts line the dining-room walls; there's
even a depression-era mural along the back wall depicting the
same splendid view of the Mississippi just outside the restaurant doors (the view is virtually unchanged), painted by a wandering gypsy named Alberto in return for food and lodging.
See if you can spot the tiny yellow biplane Alberto painted
against his blue Midwestern sky.

Jacob Breitbach, Mike's great-great-grandfather, purchased
the 1852 tavern in 1891, and it's been in the Breitbach family
ever since. (Mike and his wife, Cindy, are at the restaurant
almost all the time to greet you, chat about some of the memorabilia, and invite you to sign the guest book.) Some of the
most fascinating artifacts in the restaurant are from Jacob's
era, including a horse blanket left in the livery stable by Frank
James, Jesse James's clearly forgetful brother, and an important member of his bank- and train-robbing gang. Great-great-
grandpa Jacob actually had the foresight to take a picture of
the James gang when they stopped in at Breitbach's back in
1876, and the old photograph now hangs on the wall.

Many of the items you see in the restaurant are for sale, but
these James-gang articles are Breitbach keepers, so take a good
close look before you leave. And take a real close look at the
surliest-looking one of the bunch in the photograph. Isn't that
Jesse James giving brother Frank rabbit ears?

Breitbach's is located north of Dubuque on the Great River
Road. Take U.S. Highway 52 out of Dubuque to Sageville and
then follow the Great River Road into Balltown. Breitbach's will

be on the right. For the summer season Breitbach's is open for breakfast, lunch, and dinner seven days a week. During winter, it's closed Monday. For information and reservations call (563) 552–2220.

THE GEYSER DOWNTOWN
Belle Plaine

For better or worse, towns usually don't get to choose their claims to fame. Sure, it's nice to be home to a famous athlete, or Nobel Prize winner, or even a politician, in a pinch, but unfortunately all towns can't be so lucky. Belle Plaine's moment (or months) in the national and international spotlights came on August 26, 1886, when an artesian well dug by William Weir & Sons spouted water 53 feet in the air and kept on flowing unchecked for the next fourteen months. News reports from the time claim the well was "vomiting out a stream as large as the fore wheel of a wagon," and though we're not sure how big a fore wheel is, we know it's got to be a whole lot bigger than a breadbox, but maybe smaller than the back wheel of a wagon.

One thing is certain about the well, aptly christened Jumbo: It sent a whole lot of water into Belle Plaine. According to experts Jumbo Well spewed more than 5 million gallons of water daily, or about 3,500 gallons per minute, which, in case you were curious, calculates to about sixty gallons a second. (Try taking a sip from the flow, and the phrase "a stiff drink" would gain a whole new meaning.) In case you're not good with figures, that's a lot of water, so much, in fact, that William Weir & Sons, the men who drilled the well, watched the torrent of water erupt before them, tried for a few desperate hours to

*You wouldn't know it now, but this quiet corner
was once home to a very stubborn geyser.*

do something about it, and then left town by early evening—
townsfolk assumed they were going to get more specialized
equipment to stop the geyser—never to return.

And as the water kept on flowing, Belle Plaine's fame grew.
Tourists from around the country and around the world came
to see Jumbo, bought postcards of the gusher (now only 6 or 7
feet high, at least in the postcard we saw) and commemorative
Jumbo Well rocks, and did whatever else one did in nineteenth-
century Belle Plaine. In spite of the benefits of the friendly visitors and their greenbacks, Belle Plaine's citizens still wanted
their five-million-gallon-a-day spigot downtown shut off, so
they brought in experts from Chicago and beyond to help, but
no one was successful. Ultimately, a local company, Palmer

Brothers Foundry, capped Jumbo on October 6, 1887, using a contraption composed of two metal pipes, one inside the other, and a whole lot of gravel and concrete. (Don't ask us how it worked; we're not engineers.)

The place where Jumbo Well once gushed is now a quiet, shady street corner in a residential neighborhood a couple of blocks from downtown Belle Plaine, with the well site marked by a large boulder and plaque. The town also honors its artesian heritage with a yearly fall festival called Jumbo Days, featuring a cemetery walk (more festive than you might think), a Fly-In Breakfast at the local airport, and a hot-air-balloon lift-off. And though a gusher that bubbled on and on and on is not a terrible thing to be famous for, a movie-star daughter or an astronaut son would have been a lot less of a headache.

The Jumbo Well boulder and plaque is located on the corner of Eighth Street and Eighth Avenue in Belle Plaine. Jumbo Days is held on the last weekend in September. For more information, contact the Belle Plaine Historical Society.

A PIT STOP AT YOUR GREAT-GRANDFATHER'S GAS STATION
Belle Plaine

The Old Lincoln Highway, the first transcontinental roadway in the United States, began in New York, ended in San Francisco 3,331 long and dusty miles later, and just so happened to pass through little Belle Plaine along the way. If you want to get a good feel for what it was like to make a pit stop for gas along the Lincoln Highway almost eighty years ago, take 21 North about 3 blocks out of town, put your right-turn blinker on, and ease the old jalopy into George Preston's gas station and garage. No brightly lit convenience store filled with

You can't fill 'er up here but take a gander at those signs. Photo: Catherine Cole

3,000 kinds of confectionary delights, no pay-at-the-pump convenience here, just a one-bay wooden garage, and, next to it, the tiny office with two old gas pumps out front, all looking pretty much the way they did back in the 1920s, save for a little graying and weathering to let you know it's all real, not some museum reproduction.

The old gas pump is worth the visit all by itself—towering almost 10 feet in the air, it looks something like a miniature lighthouse with a long, black hose attached—but George Preston also covered his station walls with hundreds of oil and gas signs from the last century. In addition to the more familiar Shell, Pennzoil, Texaco, and Mobil logos, there are signs for Red Crown (picturing a brilliant red crown, of course), Wadhams, and Nevrnox gasoline. They're a collector's fantasy and a credit to Iowa honesty and uprightness that they haven't been taken under cover of darkness and auctioned off on eBay.

Be sure to stop inside the office, too. There's an old register, fifty-year-old unopened oil cans on the shelves, newspaper clippings featuring George grinning wide for the camera beside his station, actual chunks of the old highway on the windowsill (the labels stuck on with duct tape), a poster listing the hundreds of towns the Old Lincoln Highway passed through, and even more signs, these ones offering cheery road advice such as DIM YOUR LIGHTS BEHIND A CAR, LET FOLKS SEE HOW BRIGHT YOU ARE. Stop for five minutes and spend half the afternoon as we did. Just don't blame us if you feel deep twinges of nostalgia for the good old days the next time you fill 'er up on the interstate.

Preston's gas station is at the intersection of Fourth and Thirteenth Streets, Belle Plaine.

R EAD 'E M , W EEP , AND C ALL THE M OVERS
Bellevue

Although this decidedly upscale bed-and-breakfast, located on a nine-acre wooded bluff overlooking the Mississippi, has a lot to recommend it, including a breathtaking view, twelve beautifully appointed guest rooms, and more Jacuzzi tubs than a California spa, its most notable charm is its checkered past. The Mont Rest B&B's most recent change in fortune, a devastating 1996 fire in which five fire companies unleashed more than 200,000 gallons of water to quell the flames, may not have even been its most dramatic. (Just in case you're worried about water-logged mattresses, the current innkeeper, Christine Zraick, rebuilt and refurnished the inn after the fire and returned it to its original splendor.)

Does anyone know the number for Gambler's Anonymous?

When a wealthy land developer named Seth Luellyn Baker built the home in 1893, its unique architectural feature was a round, third-floor tower room, accessible only by stepping onto the roof of the building and then climbing through a hatch. The room's purpose? High-stakes, invitation-only, illegal (because transpiring on land) poker matches, conducted safe from the intrusions of the local authorities. Mont Rest quickly grew infamous for its late-night gambling, and it was in one of these heavyweights-only poker matches in 1895, just two years after Mont Rest was built, that Seth Baker, short of cash, called a $6,000 bet with the deed to his house. Oh, and did I mention Seth Baker had a wife, a woman who probably considered the house hers, too? After his opponent lay his cards on the table, Mr. Baker is reported to have excused himself, climbed out the hatch, then walked across the roof and down the stairs to tell his beloved they had two weeks to pack up and move out. (Do you think they had couples therapy back in 1895?)

The gambling room underwent a conversion of sorts in the early twentieth century, when an eccentric owner named Frank Weinshank set up an altar and heard daily Mass in the tower from a local priest. One of Weinshank's more eccentric acts, in a lifetime filled with kookiness, was filing a lawsuit against Bell Telephone for religious persecution for refusing to lay a transatlantic phone line from Mont Rest to the Vatican in Rome so that he could have a direct line to the pope. You don't need to be William Rehnquist to know his case had a few holes in it.

To top it all off, from the fifties until the late seventies, Mont Rest and the Tower Room, as it's now called, stood abandoned: Animals took up residence, vandals smashed windows, and the woods encroached on the property. As recently as 1979, the *Des Moines Register* ran a story about the so-called Haunted Castle of Bellevue, which loomed on the north bluff overlooking town.

And now Mont Rest is arguably one of the most luxurious bed-and-breakfasts in the region. Guests can reserve the Tower Room if they're looking for privacy, a sweeping view of the river, rich history, a double shower, and just outside on the roof where gamblers once strode, a seven-person hot tub. Seth Baker, even when he was on the winning side of the table, probably never had it so good.

Bellevue is located midway between Clinton and Dubuque on US 52 (the Great River Road). Mont Rest's address is 300 Spring Street, right on the bluff 3 blocks north of downtown. Christine Zraick, the innkeeper, can be reached toll-free at (877) 872–4220 or (563) 872–4220.

CHECK OUT THE IOWA CZECHS
Cedar Rapids

*E*ven though they rank as the two biggest cities in northeastern Iowa, Cedar Rapids and Iowa City don't seem
much like cities at all. No traffic jams, no interstates twisted
together like giant concrete Christmas ribbons, and no sky-
scrapers, unless you'd call a twenty-two-story building (the
tallest building in Cedar Rapids) a skyscraper.

That's not to say Cedar Rapids and Iowa City are cut from
the same small-city mold. It's hard to imagine two places in
Iowa more distinct in character and vibe. Home to the University of Iowa, with a student enrollment around 27,000, and the
University of Iowa Hospitals and Clinics, considered one of
"America's Best Hospitals," Iowa City oozes bookishness (and
bookstores). Cedar Rapids, home to both Quaker Oats, the
largest cereal manufacturer in the world, and APAC, the
nation's largest asphalt and concrete paving company, has a
decidedly industrial feel. How industrial you might ask? More
than 190 manufacturing plants in the city collectively employ
about 22,000 people.

That 1930s industrial vibe in Cedar Rapids, with old neigh-
borhoods bumping up against nearby factories, underlies much
of its charm. You can just imagine a 1950s Dad waving good-
bye to Mom and the kids as he carries his lunch pail down the
street to clock in. If you're looking for more charm, then cross
the bridge to City Hall. Cedar Rapids claims the unique honor
of being the only city in the world other than Paris to have its
municipal buildings on an island in the city center (May's
Island, in the middle of the Cedar River).

There's even an ethnic neighborhood called Czech Village, a
sort of dollhouse version of Wicker Park, Chicago, and
arguably the best part of Cedar Rapids. More than 22 percent

of the population of Cedar Rapids is of Czech descent, and this is where a good number of their ancestors first lived. The neighborhood consists of 4 or 5 square blocks of pre–World War II buildings and working-class homes that have thankfully escaped gentrification. At present there's a Czech baker, a Czech restaurant, and a store that sells imported Czech glass. And, since Iowans love their museums as much as they love education, there's also a Czech and Slovak Museum to give you the historical view.

If you're not in the mood for edification, though, just wander the streets around the Salvation Army, the ambience epicenter of Czech Village, and dig those industrial and postindustrial vibes.

The Salvation Army is just before the old bridge over the Cedar River, at Sixteenth Avenue. Czech Village extends 5 blocks in all directions.

CLARK GABLE, SHAKESPEARE, AND HOME MOVIES
Cedar Rapids

Drive down Cedar Rapids' busy First Avenue, look to the east, and there, amid commercial buildings and modest homes, floats a vision from another time and place: an English mansion. Built between 1884 and 1886 by Caroline Sinclair, the widow of the city's first meatpacking baron, the Queen Anne–style mansion was called "the grandest house west of Chicago." Brucemore, this three-story, twenty-one-room building sits on twenty-seven acres of parklike estate and boasts clustering gables, bay and oriel windows, turrets, porches, and magnificent chimney caps. At present a tour of the building sheds light on the upper-crust ways of its three owners—the

Sinclairs (1884–1906), the Douglases (1906–1937), and the Halls (1937–1981)—as well as on the many workers and domestic doers who made the owners' leisure lives possible.

The Hall Film Library, a collection of 16-mm films shot by Howard Hall, the mansion's third owner, contains a three-minute, behind-the-scenes clip from the set of *Gone with the Wind*, the only known footage of its kind from the legendary film. The home movie captures the opening scene, the barbecue at Twelve Oaks, with highlights that include Clark Gable and Vivian Leigh sitting by their trailers in full costume, smoking cigarettes as they wait for their scenes. Some shots reveal hundreds of extras in antebellum costumes, standing motionless in the hot California sun, just waiting for the director to call out, "Action!"

Brucemore is at 2160 Linden Drive SE, Cedar Rapids. For more information call (319) 362–7375. It's open for tours year-round, but during summer the mansion hosts Shakespeare on the Lawn, a delightful way to spend the evening in this city more famous for oatmeal than art. Seventeenth-century English theater for Cedar Rapidians on the lawn of their very own English mansion: What could be stranger or more strangely fitting?

CSPS: ARTSY SOHO MEETS CEDAR RAPIDS
Cedar Rapids

What do you do with a Czech social hall after the Czechs move out? The answer: Turn it into one of the most avant-garde music, theater, and art spaces in the Midwest. Its official name is Legion Arts, but most people know it by the name of the three-story brick building it occupies, CSPS, short for the Czech and Slovak Prudential Society Hall, built in 1897 and listed on the National Register of Historic Places.

Artists Mel Andringa and F. John Herbert founded CSPS more than a decade ago with the goal of showcasing young artists, cutting-edge theater, and experimental art forms for the community, and since then they've hosted up to a dozen art exhibits and sixty-five performance-art events a season. With two large galleries, a 150-seat theater, a talented and hard-working staff, and a shoestring budget, CSPS has managed to attract some of the hottest artists and performers in the country (and in a dozen other countries) to downtown Cedar Rapids, just a stone's throw from the Quaker Oats Factory. Sound unlikely? Then check out an exhibit or performance for yourself and support one of the hippest art organizations in the heartland.

CSPS is at 1103 Third Street SE. Open every day from noon to after that night's show.

THE SECRET IS IN THE SAUCE
Cedar Rapids

Whether he was maintaining journalistic objectivity or not, a reporter from the Chicago *Sun Times* once noted, "Searching for the best soul food in Iowa is like looking for a square dance in Harlem." Well, he obviously didn't look too hard in Cedar Rapids, because Al and Irene's has long been *the* place to go in eastern Iowa for anyone seeking a soul-food fix. Al and Irene Quarterman claim their family barbecue sauce dates back more than seventy years; they slather it on chicken, pork, back ribs, spareribs, beef ribs, and even turkey, and then they serve it up right, with a healthy dollop of coleslaw. Save some room for dessert, too—they make their own delectable

*Barbeque this good will make you feel like you've
died and gone to Chicago.*

pies from scratch. So where exactly did you say that square
dance was in Harlem?

Al and Irene's is located east of I–380 near Blair's Ferry
Road at 2020 Northtown Lane NE. Hours of operation are
Sunday, Tuesday, Wednesday, Thursday, 11:00 A.M.–9:00 P.M.;
Friday and Saturday, 11:00 A.M.–10:00 P.M.; closed Monday.

How Strange, a Prairie in Iowa
Chester

I t may seem strange, but in a place that used to be nothing but prairie, people can now live their whole lives without ever seeing one. The flowers and prairie grass that at one time blanketed the state grew so high that as one nineteenth-century soldier-explorer said, you could tie the stalks together over the back of a horse. In the prairie's stead, of course, we now have hundreds of thousands of acres of corn, soy, and oats that

Bet you never thought you'd see a real prairie in Iowa.

eventually end up in everything from breakfast cereals to soft drinks to internal-combustion engines. But as beautiful as those rows and rows of corn can be, the way the gaps between the stalks suddenly open into slivers of shadow and then just as quickly close as you're driving by, the prairie is the Iowa countryside's wilder, more extravagant incarnation.

If you've never seen a prairie, then be sure to visit 240-acre Hayden Prairie, one of the largest in the state. The parcel of land is really the size of a single small farm, but it's big enough so that if you walk far enough out into the tall grasses, the gravel roads and fences disappear from view, and you can easily imagine what it was like here 160 years ago, when pioneers just started the backbreaking work of turning prairie into farmland. Though the countless varieties of flowers and grasses growing and blooming—from big bluestem to purple prairie clover to yellow star grass—will vary with the season, the prairie is profligate, and wildly beautiful, from early spring to autumn. Just a word of caution from our lawyers, though: Tying prairie grass around a horse's back is not recommended by the authors, as serious injuries, and grass stains, could result.

Hayden Prairie is a few miles south of Chester on County Road V26.

A One-Horse, Two-Tractor Town
Clermont

This small town, population 716, located midway between Postville and West Union on U.S. Highway 18, is blessed with not one but two famous (at least by Iowa standards) tractors. Both tractors sit conveniently on Main Street about 1 block apart in small, simple wooden buildings with large plate-glass windows facing the street for easy viewing. There's no admission charge, no lines, and the night we visited, not a single other adult downtown, just three kids playing tag in the middle of the quiet street.

The first, and perhaps most famous, tractor, is the green 1966 John Deere riding lawn mower and absurdly large attached trailer (complete with small set of antlers up front) featured in the 1999 David Lynch film, *The Straight Story*. Based on a true story, the film chronicles the adventures of Alvin Straight, a seventy-three-year-old retiree from Laurens, Iowa, who, having lost his driver's license because of poor eyesight, decides to drive his lawn mower more than 260 miles across two states to visit his estranged and ailing brother in Mount Zion, Wisconsin. Along the way he meets a pregnant runaway, a fellow World War II vet, and a priest, among others, and there's plenty of heartwarming straight talk between Alvin and his fellow Iowans; when someone asks why he's driving a tractor, at a top speed of 5 miles per hour, all the way to Wisconsin, he says simply, "My eyes are bad. I can't drive. I don't like someone else driving. And I've got to get out to my brother." Spoken like a true Iowan.

The second tractor, though less famous, is still impressive. It's a 1927 Hart Parr manufactured in Charles City, Iowa. Now the rusting machine sits on a faded purple shag carpet—a keepsake from the tractor's 1970s disco phase?—looking exactly like what it is: a very old tractor. The manufacturer of the machine, Hart Parr, is famous for having first coined the term *tractor* when the company shortened the old name for the machines, Gasoline Traction Engines. The information posted beside the tractor kindly explains, IT HAS A TWO CYLINDER, FOUR CYCLE, HORIZONTAL VALVE IN-HEAD ENGINE, and if you know what that means, then you're either a farmer or a good candidate for a very old tractor repair school.

The tractors are located on Main Street (US 18) in downtown Clermont.

Help! Help! Rescue That Seed!
Decorah

ver try a Cherokee Purple Tomato or a White Wonder
Cucumber? Ever sampled Jimmy Nardello's Sweet Italian
Frying Peppers (that's quite a mouthful), sunk your teeth into
a delicious ear of Bloody Butcher Corn, with its dark, wine-red
kernels, or tasted some Rattlesnake Snap Beans? If your
answers were no, no, no, no, and no, it's not surprising, especially if you pick your veggies from the local megagrocery-
store produce aisles, where hybrid vegetables bred to withstand
long hauls from places as far away as New Zealand and Chile
are the norm. (Them skins are made for transcontinental ship-
ping.)

All of the above qualify as heirlooms, rare varieties of vegetables, fruits, and grains handed down within families of gardeners for generations. But unlike the family jewels, these
heirlooms are available to everyone, from weekend gardeners
to commercial growers, in a free catalog published by the Seed
Saver's Exchange, a Decorah-based nonprofit dedicated to saving more than 11,000 endangered varieties of garden seeds
from extinction. Founded in 1975, the Seed Saver's Exchange,
or SSE, has more than 8,000 members, some of whom grow
their own heirloom varieties and make the seeds available to
the SSE and the public.

The Seed Saver's Exchange also owns and operates the
beautiful 170-acre Heritage Farm near Decorah, which serves
as heirloom-vegetable patch, rare-fruit orchard, and headquar-
ters for the organization. They offer daily tours of both Preservation Gardens and Historic Orchard throughout the growing
season, where visitors might see such colorful varieties as
Boothby's Blonde Cucumbers, Applegreen Eggplants, or Black
Sea Man Tomatoes. You may want to visit in mid- to late July,

Help! Help! Save that purple tomato!

when the gardens are literally bursting with fruits and vegetables, many of which have longer pedigrees than Kentucky thoroughbreds. Besides learning about various garden-plant histories, you'll also discover that heirloom fruits and vegetables offer benefits including superior taste, staggered ripening, resistance against crop diseases, and greater variety of flavors, colors, and shapes. But before you go, be forewarned: All those poor endangered plants can really tug at the old heartstrings. If you're tempted to save a threatened variety by buying twenty-five pounds of, say, Taponica Striped Maize seed (those purple stripes on the corn leaves are beautiful, aren't they?), you could regret it come planting time.

The Seed Saver's Exchange Heritage Farm, 3076 North Winn Road, Decorah, is open for daily tours Memorial Day to October from 9:00 A.M. to 5:00 P.M. From the junction of Highway 9 and US 52, drive 5.5 miles north on US 52. Turn right on North Winn Road (W–34) and proceed 1 mile to the visitor parking sign. For more information call (563) 382–5990.

A L   C A P O N E ' S   H I D E A W A Y
D u b u q u e

E very gangster needs a little down time, a chance to leave behind the general mayhem and upheaval of the whole racketeering racket. Even as famously tough a mobster as Al "Scarface" Capone needed a weekend getaway, a place to take a holiday from the daily grind of bribing, threatening, extorting, embezzling, maiming, and killing. And, of course, where else would he go when the rat race in Chicago got him down but Iowa?

And the digs he chose to help him get back into killer form? Downtown Dubuque's own Julien Inn. A luxury hotel has stood at 200 Main Street since 1839, when it was one of the largest buildings in Dubuque and the first structure people saw crossing the Mississippi from the east. In 1889 Dubuque was almost as populous as Chicago, and the Julien was the city's Ritz Carlton, a focal point of well-to-do socializing and negotiating. Capone is reputed to have owned the Julien during prohibition and used it as a personal hideaway; some historians even claim he had an underground garage nearby where he kept his personal cars hidden from view. Others speculate that Capone owned or supplied bootlegged liquor to numerous speakeasies in East Dubuque, a place so committed to hard drinking that the news of Prohibition brought riots in the streets.

Mirror in the lobby of the Julien, where Scarface might have checked the part in his hair. Photo: Catherine Cole

Now, the Julien Inn is a modestly priced but very well-appointed hotel, featuring vintage photos of Dubuque on the corridor walls, a beautiful lobby, complete with fountain, Ziegfeld mirror, and old barbershop chair and sink, where male patrons, Capone perhaps among them, used to be able to get a shave and a haircut. (Pity the poor barber who had to carefully shave his way around that scar.) Even if you're not into busting heads and bootlegging, you can still take Capone's lead and relax at the Julien Inn. Capone famously said, "You can go a long way with a smile, but you can go a lot further with a smile and a gun," but hotel management assures us smiles are more than sufficient to inspire the staff to help at the Julien.

The Julien Inn is located in the historic Old Main Street district, 200 Main Street. For more information and reservations, call (563) 546–8867.

FOR THE LOVE OF THE NAP
Dubuque

Though Dubuque's Fenelon Place Elevator, or Fourth Street Elevator as it's also known, may possibly be the steepest, shortest railroad in the world, it's most certainly the only railroad ever built so that a person could enjoy an afternoon nap.

In 1882 it took Dubuque resident J. K. Graves, a former mayor and Iowa senator, about half an hour to drive his horse and buggy from his home on top of the bluffs to the bank where he worked at the bottom, even though the actual distance between the two was the equivalent of a mere 2½ very, very steep blocks, straight down the bluff. Not a terrible commute by present-day standards, but with only an hour and a half for lunch, during which time the whole town shut down (was Dubuque settled by Spaniards perhaps, to have such long lunches?), Mr. Graves didn't have enough time to get up the bluff, eat his lunch, take his preferred half-hour nap, and get back to the bank for business. (I know what you're thinking: Poor, poor Mr. Graves. Why doesn't he try scarfing down a ham sandwich bought from a vending machine as he sits multitasking in some windowless cubicle like the rest of us?)

Instead of buying a faster horse or forfeiting a minute of his precious siesta, Graves decided to build a 296-foot cable-car line to pull him up and down the 189-foot-high bluff. Mr. Graves's horse put in for early retirement on July 24, 1882, the cable car operated for the first time the following day, and a mere few days later (or so it must have seemed) J. K. Graves's neighbors began pestering him to ride the elevator, too. He opened the elevator to the public in 1884, charging 5 cents a ride, and soon townspeople were depending on it to get them to work, to church, to school, and to their own afternoon naps.

The view from the top of Fenelon Place Elevator.
Photo: Catherine Cole

Originally a wooden Swiss-style car hauled up and down two rails using a coal-fired steam engine, a winch, and a hemp rope, the Fenelon Place Elevator caught fire a few times and went through a number of mechanical incarnations. Now, the elevator is composed of two small, glass-enclosed counterbalanced cars, three rails (with a fourth-rail bypass in the middle of the bluff to allow the cars to pass each other), and a gearbox with a DC motor. The bluff is steep, the ride is pleasantly slow, and the view of the city and the river beyond opens up very, very quickly as you ascend. If you enter from the bottom of the bluff, at Fourth Street, you simply get on the car, ring the bell, and wait to ascend; you pay the fare ($1.50 round trip for adults, 50 cents for children) at the operator's house up top, where there's also a deck for enjoying the view. But, alas, there's no lunch waiting for you, as there would have been for Graves, and there's certainly no bed available to the public for napping. Could someone at least pass a Lunchable?

The Fenelon Place Elevator is located at 512 Fenelon Place, on top of the bluff overlooking town. You can also board a car from Fourth Street, at the bottom of the bluff, and then pay at the top. The elevator is open April 1 through November 30, 8:00 A.M. to 10:00 P.M. For more information call (563) 582–6496.

FARMERS AND THEIR TOYS
Dyersville

I f the wisdom on bumper stickers is true, and those with the most toys truly do win, then the National Farm Toy Museum in Dyersville is the winner many times over. With two floors of more than 30,000 farm toys and exhibits, ranging from row after row of common tractors to combines, harvesters, and haulers, all the way down the extensive agricultural machinery lineup to the anhydrous ammonia tanker, the museum is a shrine in miniature to the heavy equipment Iowa farmers cuss at, fuss over, endlessly fix, periodically live in (during planting and harvesting), and tirelessly operate to bring home the grain or the beans that bring home the bacon.

And don't let the word *toy* fool you—the only thing toylike about these farm toys is that they're built to $\frac{1}{16}$ or $\frac{1}{32}$ scale and don't have internal-combustion engines. This is Iowa, after all, and farm machines aren't child's play, even when they're toys. Most of the toys are stunningly accurate, not to mention beautiful, replicas of tractors or combines from particular makers— like John Deere and Case—from particular years, with details accurate down to the windshield wipers. Children playing with these toys not only got to have fun, they got a vocational education in heavy equipment.

Highlights of the museum include an exhibit explaining the notion of scale that features a full-sized replica of a John Deere tractor accompanied by a row of successively smaller scale models, from ½ scale all the way down to a realistic-looking tractor you can carry in your pocket. Upstairs look for more tractors and harvesters enclosed in glass cases, more, perhaps, than you ever hoped to see, but also check out the exhibit that details the history of grain harvesting, from Native American farmers and their hand methods to the first horse-drawn, steam-powered harvesters, down the centuries to the current cushioned-seat, air-conditioned-cab behemoths.

And though the word *toy* does, technically, appear in this museum's name, don't expect much playing around here. Tractors, trucks, trailers, and combines, even at ½₂ or even ¼₄ scale, are way too wrapped up in Iowa's blood, sweat, and sorrow to be simple objects of play. Don't be surprised if you see some old-timer kicking the tires of a tiny Case Combine, wondering how it'd hold up more than 2,000 acres, or some young 'un quietly cussing a pocket-sized John Deere because it won't turn over.

The National Farm Toy Museum is at the intersection of US 20 and Highway 136 in Dyersville. Open daily from 8:00 A.M. to 7:00 P.M., the museum also hosts a number of special shows and exhibits throughout the year, the largest of which is the "granddaddy of all farm toy shows," held the first full weekend of November. For more information call (319) 875–2727.

HOLLYWOOD DREAMIN' IN IOWA
Dyersville

Even though Iowa has no professional baseball team, over the last fourteen years almost a million people from all over the world have come to visit a small ballpark just outside Dyersville. And even though the ballpark is almost as famous as Fenway, no vendors walk up and down the bleachers yelling "Buuudwizah! Buuudwizah!," no rabid fans fill out their scorecards and scream at the ump, and, most surprisingly, players rarely ever take the field for a real game (and when they do, they're usually ghost players).

In 1989 *Field of Dreams* was filmed on the ninety-one-year-old Lansing family farm just outside Dyersville after the Iowa Film Board pitched it to Hollywood as the perfect spot for a movie about a farmer, Ray Kinsella (played by Kevin Costner), who turns a portion of his acreage into a baseball diamond after hearing a voice and having visions. Some insiders even claim that in addition to circulating a beautiful photograph of the Lansing farmhouse, the corn around it tall and greener than outfield grass, the Film Board helped make their case to the Hollywood execs by saying there were plenty of us Iowans who hear voices and have visions all the time. Sure, some Nebraskans hear voices, and some Minnesotans have visions, but Iowa has the highest percentage of farmers who hear voices and have visions at the same time. Hollywood was sold.

During filming in the summer of 1988, the house got a new wraparound porch, and the baseball field, with its Little League–size infield and telephone-pole-style lighting, was built in three days. Once the filming was over, the Lansings—and their neighbor, Al Ameskamp, who happened to own the center-

The ball field that a hallucinating farmer built.
Photo: Catherine Cole

and left-field property—hadn't even had a chance to convert the land back to tillage before tourists started showing up to get a look at the real Field of Dreams. And once the farmers saw that more than 50,000 people a year would visit, with money burning holes in their pockets, it didn't take the neighbors long to start feuding. The end result is that there are two proprietors, two driveways, and two competing souvenir stands at the Field of Dreams, one called (appropriately if a bit unimaginatively) Left & Center Field of Dreams, peddling its wares along the third-base line, and the other called simply Field of Dreams, with its booth at the top of the Lansing's driveway.

For all the red-blooded American economic competition at
the site, the place remains largely true to the simple, nostalgic
spirit of the movie—Field of Dreams and Left & Center Field of
Dreams together comprise a small baseball field in the corn
beside a quaint-looking farmhouse. Families keep coming, summer after summer, to play catch, hit a few balls, and see where
a baseball film that captured their hearts and imaginations was
made. Even a little old-fashioned litigation between neighbors
can't spoil something as simple as that.

Dyersville is just off U.S. Highway 20, about 25 miles west
of Dubuque. To get to the Field of Dreams, head north out of
town on Highway 136, cross the railroad tracks, and then take
a right onto Third Avenue NE. From there it's about 4 miles to
the field; just follow the signs. Open daily April through
November, 9:00 A.M. to 6:00 P.M. The last Sunday of each
month, June through September, from noon to 2:00 P.M., the
Ghost Players (some of whom appeared in the original movie)
step from the corn and play ball, re-creating one of the most
poignant scenes in the film. Call (563) 875–6012 or (563)
875–8404 for more information.

TIE A YELLOW RIBBON 'ROUND THE OLD STONE MAN
Fayette

Just west of Fayette at a T intersection on a gravel road,
perched on a small concrete slab among the grasses and
wildflowers between the roadbed and rows of corn, sits one of
the county's most famous residents—the Stone Man. Only 3½
feet tall but weighing in at an impressive one-half ton, the
Stone Man is really a granite boulder vaguely resembling a
human (why Stone Man and not Stone Woman, we're not sure),

A little man who once had a big wardrobe.
Photo: Catherine Cole

in much the same way a cloud can resemble Richard Nixon's profile. There's a certain rough resemblance for your imagination to work with, but not a whole lot of verisimilitude.

And therein lies the Stone Man's charm. Sitting in his humble drainage ditch, half-obscured by weeds, he looks like the forgotten work of some prehistoric sculptor. Unlike slightly more famous American rock landmarks, like Mount Rushmore, Crazy Horse, and the former Old Man on the Mountain, the Stone Man's crude form, tiny size, and utter lack of pretension (just a small plaque identifies him), can make suckers for the underdog like me swoon at his feet, or, more truthfully, his wide, footless, legless base, as he seems to be wearing a long, flowing cloak, actually, which obscures his arms, feet, and legs as well as every other part of his body.

He's the kind of 3-foot Stone Man who makes you want to take him home and mother him.

Not much is known about the Stone Man, which only adds to his appeal, of course—everyone loves a man of mystery. Where did he come from? What purpose, if any, did he serve? Levern and Jo Ellen Knight, local historians and resident experts on the Stone Man, have done extensive research but have come up with only unsubstantiated theories, the most interesting of which is that the Stone Man served as a boundary marker between early settler and Indian lands. From historical accounts they discovered that the Stone Man has been used as a meeting spot and guidepost for travelers as far back as the 1880s. Settlers would give directions by saying things like, "Drive your team past a whole lot of corn, and when you get to the Stone Man, bang a right and you're almost there." Farm families would often meet at the Stone Man before heading into town for church or shopping, but if one family decided not to wait for the others, they'd tie father's necktie around the Stone Man, or place mother's bonnet on his head as a sign that they'd gone ahead. According to some accounts the Stone Man sported a different piece of clothing almost every day of summer and therefore appeared to have one of the most extensive wardrobes in the county. And, although we can't ever be certain of this, he was probably one of the only men in the county to regularly sport a church bonnet.

Head north out of Fayette on Highway 150 about half a mile to the top of the hill and then take a left onto 152nd Street. Travel west on 152nd for about 2 miles until it ends at M Street. At the intersection look to the left and you'll see the Stone Man peeking up from the grasses or the snow, depending on the time of year.

CHURCH FOR EIGHT (OR A CROWDED TWELVE)
Festina

We might as well get the bitter truth out of the way up front: though many people claim St. Anthony of Padua Chapel in Festina to be the "World's Smallest Church" (including my Iowa Department of Transportation Map), it is most certainly not. Just to give one example, at 12 by 16 feet, St. Anthony's is significantly larger than the so-called "Smallest Church in America" in South Newport, Georgia, which measures 10 by 15 feet. And the people way down in Georgia may be excused for never having heard of the much smaller 4-by-6-foot chapel in Oneida, New York, with just enough room for minister, bride, groom, and perhaps one very small flower girl.

But you don't even need to go all the way to Oneida to raise serious doubts about Festina's littlest church claims. An argument can be made (though we wouldn't make it) that it's not even the smallest chapel in eastern Iowa, since Palmer College, the chiropractic school in Davenport, has an 8-by-8-by-10-foot chapel on campus dedicated to the memory of Mr. Palmer, the founder of chiropractic medicine. Last time we checked, though, Mr. Palmer still hadn't been canonized for bringing relief to the spinally afflicted.

Even though the St. Anthony of Padua Chapel has a monstrous (by small church standards) 30-foot steeple, a regular-size door, and comfortable seating for eight to twelve thin Iowans, the chapel somehow still gained some measure of fame as the "Smallest Church in the World." Was it a Festina Chamber of Commerce conspiracy to suppress information about smaller chapels worldwide? A case of local pride winning out against the hard facts? Or just good old-fashioned hometown

The littlest church on the prairie.

boosterism? Whatever the reason, whether innocent or diaboli-
cal, the church is frequently, but usually unofficially, referred
to as the "World's Smallest Church."

Even if it's not a world-record-holder, the church is still very small and quite charming, in the way that mini versions of commonly large things can be. Built in 1885 by Mary Ann and Frank Joseph Huber to fulfill a promise by Mary Ann's grandmother to build a church if her son returned home safely from war, the church contains four robin's-egg-blue pews, four simple stained-glass windows, and a tiny altar with a statue of St. Anthony. Located on quiet, tree-shaded grounds, surrounded by some of the most beautiful (not to mention fertile) farms in the world, the church may not be the smallest around, but it's certainly got to be one of the prettiest.

Thankfully, most official information and signage for the church makes no world-record claims, once again confirming Iowans as more or less trustworthy folk. The small blue signs directing you down gravel roads past rolling green hills and Swiss Valley–owned dairy farms to St. Anthony's say simply LITTLEST CHURCH. Not LITTLEST CHURCH IN THE WORLD or LITTLEST CHURCH IN AMERICA or even LITTLEST CHURCH AROUND THESE PARTS— just plain LITTLEST CHURCH. Potentially misleading? Yes. A lie? Not really. They're signs a politician could stand behind, and that's good enough for us.

Take 123rd Street west out of Festina about 2 miles. Take a left on Little Church Road (NOTE: Here's an honest sign—the church is, in fact, little). St. Anthony of Padua Chapel is about 1 mile down on the left.

THE ONLY SHOPPING IN TOWN
Garrison

The Farmer's Mercantile in downtown Garrison may not have much of a selection. For example, the store carries only two kinds of breakfast cereal: Rice Krispies and Corn

Flakes—but it has at least one thing no one else does: eighty-year-old Emma Croswell, owner and proprietor. A no-nonsense woman with lively eyes and a winning smile, Emma has worked at the store for sixty-two years, selling local farm families everything from fuel oil to men's overalls to ice cream. And she still comes in six days a week to sell groceries and odds and ends, though these days hours and hours can pass without a single customer.

No town booster, Emma's frank about the changes Garrison has gone through over the last few decades. "This town's going downhill," she says, pointing to the boarded-up ground-floor windows of the building across the street. "Look at that plywood—that won't hold up." On living in the same small town all her life, Emma says, "Someone called me the other day and said, 'Emma, are we cousins?' and I said, 'I don't know, maybe third or fourth.' And she said, 'My son's been looking it up and he says we are.' So I guess we are." When I naively replied by saying it must be nice having so many relatives in town, Emma said matter-of-factly, "Maybe it's good . . . maybe it's not so good."

Emma started work at the store the day after finishing high school in 1942 and immediately earned the nickname "the Policeman" for catching customers placing extra merchandise in their orders after already having paid. "I could remember each order in my head without looking at a slip, and when there was something extra, I could tell." Back then the store was open until 10:00 P.M. each night, and her second evening on the job Emma's sharp eye saved the store $200. "You might not think people back then would steal like that, but they were no different from people today."

Nowadays $200 in shoplifting might wipe out half the store's inventory. The Farmer's Mercantile still has its old wooden dry-goods tables and glass-front cabinets, a copper ceiling, and an ornate 1918 cash register with a hand crank and wooden till, but the shelves are a little bare. There are a few children's toys along one wall, a display filled with 98-cent greeting cards, cans of soda lined up on the bakery shelves,

"The Policeman" taking a break from her patrols.

and nonperishable groceries that you'd expect to find at a camp store, including a few bottles of ketchup, a couple of jars of pickles, bags of marshmallows, and a surprisingly large stock of Jell-O.

But what the Farmer's Mercantile lacks in selection, Emma more than makes up for in conversation. She spent hours talking with me, and I bought only a Coke. In that time just one person dropped in, a regular named Bill, so frequent a customer, Emma said, that sometimes people call the store looking for him if they can't find him at home. Bill, every bit as frank as Emma, told me, "This place is definitely unique. When Emma falls over on her head, it'll be done." For the record Emma has no plans of falling on her head anytime soon. She's even thinking about hiring her one-hundred-year-old uncle from Omaha to help with the mercantile, but she's taking time to think about it. From experience Emma knows that a blood relation in such close proximity can be a mixed blessing.

Located in downtown Garrison, 100 West Main Street, the Farmer's Mercantile is open Monday through Saturday. Call ahead to be sure Emma will be there: (319) 477–3115.

H I S T O R I C   M O U N D S   w / V I E W
H a r p e r s   F e r r y

To say that European settlers are relative newcomers to Iowa is perhaps a bit of an understatement. Native peoples lived in Iowa for at least 12,000 years before we Johnny-come-latelies started building settler's log cabins about 160 years ago.

But what physical record remains of their 12,000 years here in Iowa? Native peoples weren't into large-scale agribusiness, interstate highways, or permanent dwellings, but in northeastern Iowa they left behind thousands and thousands of mysterious earthen mounds, 3 to 4 feet in height and up to 200 feet long, many of them in the shapes of birds, turtles, lizards, bison, and, most commonly, bears. Most of the mounds, unfortunately, have fallen to the plow over the last century. Surveys in the late nineteenth and early twentieth centuries documented more than 10,000 mounds in the region, but by the end of the century fewer than 1,000 remained.

Of those surviving mounds 195 are located in Effigy Mounds National Monument, a beautiful 2,526-acre park located just north of Marquette along the banks of the Mississippi. Dating from between 3,000 and 750 years ago, the mounds are one of the only records we have of the people who once flourished along the river, fishing, hunting white-tailed deer, and harvesting freshwater mussels, wild rice, acorns, and berries. The majority of the mounds are conical or linear in shape, but thirty-two of them take the form of animal effigies. At Effigy, you'll find earthen mounds in the shape of both birds and bears; one bird mound on the site has a wingspan of 212 feet, whereas the Great Bear mound is 137 feet long. Though these native inhabitants buried their dead in the conical mounds, experts aren't sure what purpose the animal-shaped mounds served, and with no written records and few surviving tribal stories, the role of the mounds in this culture is likely to remain a mystery.

A 2- or 3-mile hike through forests of oak, maple, shagbark hickory, and birch brings you past numerous animal mounds to lookout spots atop 350-foot-high bluffs with names like Hanging Rock and Fire Point, where you can take in some of the most breathtaking views of the Mississippi anywhere along its banks. Whatever the purpose of the mounds, one thing is certain: The people who built them chose prime real estate upon which to sculpt, basket load by basket load of earth, these bears and birds.

To get to Effigy Mounds, take Highway 76 north of Marquette about 3 miles. The visitor center will be on the right. Guided tours are available Memorial Day through Labor Day. For hours and days of operation, call (563) 873–3491.

FACTS ABOUT MANURE AND SOME HIGH-QUALITY HAIR ART
La Porte City

Walking into La Porte City's Future Farmers of America (FFA) Agricultural Museum is like stepping back in time into your grandparents' barn. The hallways, walls, even the ceilings are filled with antique farm tools and machinery, including hay forks, old plows, seeders, corn graters, cob driers, sheep shearers, a carriage, a broom-making machine, and a cider press. The museum seems to contain every antique farm tool imaginable (and some duplicates), but perhaps that's because the collection has outgrown its current quarters, La Porte City's old jail and adjacent firehouse. (The museum is in the process of moving to a newly renovated and larger building on Main Street.) In addition to tools the museum also contains some great old educational farm signage, including one sign charting the feed required to produce thirty dozen eggs and another with the stirring title SOME FACTS ABOUT MANURE, which offers the manure-ignorant masses whole heaps of facts, as the title promises, as well as some enlightening line art.

In case you were wondering what locals did when they weren't farming, there are also exhibits containing artifacts from virtually every aspect of the everyday, including an old dentist's office, a barbershop, a doctor's office, and a bathtub. And after harvesting the corn, milking the cows, measuring out feed to produce thirty dozen eggs, and getting their teeth pulled, some women had time left over for a fascinating pastime: braiding their own cut hair into intricate designs to be included in letters to beaus far from home. These somewhat creepy tokens of affection, resembling strips of an afghan no more than 2 or 3 inches long, are displayed in a glass case along with an envelope and a small note card claiming that the hair is on loan from a local resident.

As compelling as hair art is, if you let tour guide Lois Miszner show you her very favorite item in the collection, she'll bring you to a hardcover men's haberdashery catalog that's as big and heavy as the *Oxford English Dictionary*. Discovered inside the wall of a local home during renovation, the book was transformed by an unknown local woman into an elaborate and strikingly beautiful collage. Filled with colorful pasted pictures, postcards, and illustrations from early-twentieth-century women's magazines, this men's-clothing catalog has been converted into a record of one mysterious woman's artistic tastes and preoccupations. Unfortunately, though, she didn't seem to be into braided hair.

Currently located in the old firehouse and jail, the FFA Ag Museum is moving to 416 Main Street in downtown La Porte City. Open Saturdays and Sunday, from 1:00 to 4:00 P.M., or by appointment. Call City Hall at (319) 342–3396 for more information.

CAUTION: LARGE WAKE—
ELEPHANT WATERSKIING
Marquette

P inky, a life-sized fiberglass pink elephant, used to spend her time greeting patrons in front of the appropriately named but now defunct Pink Elephant Supper Club. Now she stands watch on Highway 76 in downtown Marquette, right in front of the casino, her long snout resting no more than 2 or 3 feet from passing traffic. The 14-foot-tall, bleary-eyed behemoth sports formal attire (a slightly askew top hat rests on her head) in order to properly welcome visitors to the Mississippi's first state-licensed gambling facility, the Miss Marquette Riverboat Casino, a barge done up in riverboat style.

Though currently a casino-industry employee, Pinky's crowning moment of glory came in August 1978, when her owner somehow coaxed her to water-ski the Mississippi at Prairie du Chien in honor of the visiting president Jimmy Carter. Was she hoping President Carter would take her on the road or just take her home to the peanut farm? Whatever motivated Pinky, it seems her hopes for more lasting glory were dashed. (Have you ever seen a pink elephant with such sad

If you think Pinky looks good now, just picture her in a wetsuit. Photo: Catherine Cole

eyes?) And since her salad days, she seems to have lost her skis, her bathing suit, and her girlish figure. Here's hoping Pinky returns to the river one day, if not to water-ski, then at least to do a little tubing.

Pinky stands watch in front of the Miss Marquette Riverboat Casino on Highway 76 in downtown Marquette.

BIRTHPLACE OF THE GREATEST
SHOW ON EARTH
McGregor

Even in a region filled with charming Mississippi River towns, from Bellevue to Guttenberg to North Buena Vista, the small town of McGregor, located just south of Marquette, is a standout. Main Street, sprinkled liberally with cafes, bookstores, inns, and antiques shops, has somehow managed to maintain its authenticity; even on days when it's crowded with out-of-towners like us, McGregor still feels like a real town rather than some tourism-dollars-obsessed reproduction of what it once was.

One of McGregor's main claims to fame is that from 1860 to 1872 it was home to August and Marie Salome Ringling and their seven boys, Albert, August (or A.G.), Otto, Alfred, Charles, John, and Henry. The boys saw their first circuses at the end of Main Street by the riverboat landing, and it wasn't long before they began putting on their own shows, raising a tent themselves in a backyard and charging a penny admission. (Anyone who's seen the Little Rascals probably has a fairly good idea of what these early "Greatest Shows on Earth" were like.) According to one eyewitness account, the performers numbered only three, two of whom offered suspiciously similar parallel-bar acts for the crowd's amusement. The highlight of the show, the same eyewitness claimed, was Al Ringling balancing a borrowed plow on his chin. The only animal, exotic or otherwise, was the town horse.

After raising money by giving exhibitions in halls and small-town theaters, five of the Ringling brothers managed to save enough money to put on their first real circus in the spring of 1884 in Baraboo, Wisconsin. The show required just nine wagons and featured no giraffes, no lions, tigers, or bears, and not a single elephant. By 1907 the Ringling brothers bought out Barnum and Bailey, and by 1929, with the purchase of the American Circus Company for $2 million, John Ringling, the last surviving brother, owned all major circus railroad shows (and a fair number of the gainfully employed elephants) in the United States.

In McGregor you can visit the former Ringling home, just a few blocks from the end of Main Street, and see where this greatest of circus dynasties began. When asked the keys to the Ringling brothers' success, brother Charles is reported to have said, "Hard work, honesty, and a keen sense of what people want." Perhaps that keen ability to know what people really want is what made the boys drop the dual parallel-bar acts and pick up some giraffes, a few leotard-clad trapeze artists, and a bunch of ferocious tigers willing to jump through flaming hoops. Pure genius.

Follow Main Street away from the river until the T intersection at Seventh Street. Take a left onto Seventh and then a right on Walton Street. The former Ringling home is 61 Walton Street. Look for the small historical marker out front.

A WOODEN-CHAIN-LOVER'S PARADISE
Monona

Small-town historical museums in Iowa are odd mixtures, one part antiques store (where the items are not for sale), one part communal attic of strange keepsakes (see La Porte City's hair art), and one part local celebrity show. For example, though the Monona Historical Museum contains the obligatory antique barber's chair, old refrigerator, and even older stove (all

Link by link, just take it link by link.

in excellent shape), it also has on display the First Monona Telephone Switchboard, a fair amount of Monona High School memorabilia, including old band uniforms and jerseys, various scary-looking items from the old area hospital, and a whole lot of hand-carved wooden chains.

For all the excitement of pulling on the switchboard cords and placing imaginary calls (it really was kind of exciting), the Monona Historical Museum's most fascinating items, of course, are the rows and rows of hand-carved wooden chains. With more than 400 chains on display in an addition built solely to house the carvings, the collection is quite honestly (and safely) hailed as the "World's Largest Known Collection of Hand Carved Chains." In other words, if there's a bigger collection out there, the museum board members sure haven't heard of it.

Local Elmer Marting Sr. began carving the chains after retiring from farming and discovering (to his dismay, we must imagine) that he didn't enjoy fishing or playing cards. What else to do, then, but carve hundreds upon hundreds of wooden chains? Elmer ended up spending a fair amount of his retirement painstakingly crafting chains from single pieces of wood using no glue, only simple carving tools and a tireless imagination for coming up with infinite variations on a theme. There are straight chains and twisted chains and chains composed of box-shaped links, some with wooden balls inside; there are teak chains and cypress chains, ironwood and burly pecan chains, coco bolo, and mulberry; there are chains carved from broom handles, from pencils (for writing chain letters, Elmer liked to say), and, miraculously, from a standard round toothpick; there's even an American flag made of wooden chains, one chain for each stripe.

Looking at all these chains, it's easy to forget that each one represents weeks of painstaking work. Though Marting enjoyed showing the chains at county fairs, he didn't sell that many, simply because the many hours of work required to make each chain made them prohibitively expensive to buy. And Elmer wasn't that interested in selling them to begin with, in part due to some shrewd thinking. Carol Marting, Elmer's daughter-in-law and one of the museum's tour guides, said that one reason Elmer donated the whole collection to the museum (after giving relatives a select few chains) was to prevent someone from selling it. "He used to say, 'If you sell them, you've got money, and when you've got money, you spend it, and after you spend it, you've got nothing.'" And 400 hand-carved chains in the hand (or hanging along four museum walls), each with its own variations and charms, are far better than nothing.

Located at 304 South Egbert Street, across the street from Monona City Park, the museum is open Sundays from 1:00 to 4:00 P.M., May 25 through October 5. It's also open by special appointment. Call Carol Marting at (563) 539–2640 to schedule a visit.

THE CHURCH BUILT BY (BUT NOT FOR) A SONG
Nashua

Find a beautiful old church in an idyllic country setting, and you can be sure people will line up months ahead of time to get hitched there. Throw a little churchly fame into the deal, though, and you've got a marriage business that might make a cash-strapped minister turn green with envy. Nashua's famous Little Brown Church in the Vale meets these criteria perfectly, and, if its annual wedding reunion the first Sunday in August is any indication—attended by as many as 500 people—the place sees as many marriages as a roadside Vegas chapel.

The church's fame is attributable to William Pitts and the four Weather-wax brothers. (Sounds like a country music act, doesn't it?) Pitts was a young music teacher who, on his way to visit his girlfriend in June of 1857, made a stagecoach pit stop beside what would one day become the Little Brown Church grounds. Moved by the beauty of the spot, the gently rolling hills, the creek, the ancient evergreens and hardwoods, he imagined how lovely a country church would look there. (Wonder why his mind was on churches. High hopes?) Upon returning home to southern Wisconsin after his visit, he wrote a

poem about his imagined church, set it to music, and titled it
"The Church in the Wildwood."

Years passed, and when Pitts eventually returned to the
area to teach music, he was shocked to see that a church was
being built in the very spot he'd imagined. His Bradford Acad-
emy vocal class sang the lines, "There's a church in the valley
by the wild-wood/No lovelier spot in the dale/No place is so dear
to my childhood as the little brown church in the vale," in public for the first time at the church's dedication in 1864. No sen-
timentalist, Pitts then sold the song to a Chicago publisher for
$25 to help finance a medical education in Chicago, but it wasn't
until decades later that the Weather-wax brothers, a popular
gospel quartet from Charles City, made the song famous by
telling Pitts's story and performing "The Church in the Wildwood" at the end of every show.

The Little Brown Church is now an interesting mix of the
religious, the secular, and the commercial. Pictures of Abraham
Lincoln and George Washington hang on the church walls;
plastic lawn ornaments sprout from the flower beds out front;
and a hotel, restaurant, and souvenir shop sit just a stone's
throw away from the church's front door. (Be sure to check out
the mini replica of the church by the bathrooms located right
behind the real church.) The grounds are quite breathtaking,
and the church is beautiful, but you don't have to look hard to
find a little Vegas here, too.

Since 1952, the Little Brown Church has hosted its annual
wedding reunion the first Sunday in August. Though it's
geared toward couples who have married at the church, the celebration is open to all. The highlight of the event is the Service
of Recommitment of the Wedding Vows, wherein couples renew
their pledges of lifelong love and fidelity. One visitor, a divorcé
who wished to remain anonymous, suggested that the Little
Brown Church hold another yearly celebration, a sort of singles party in the vale for people who didn't get it right the first
time and hope to give the Little Brown Church one, or maybe
even two, more tries.

You'll find the Little Brown Church in the Weeds
just behind the Little Brown Church in the Vale.
Photo: Catherine Cole

The Little Brown Church is located 2 miles east of Nashua on Highway 346. The church is open from early morning to evening every day, and worship service is offered each Sunday at 10:30 A.M. For more information call (641) 435–2027.

DYING FOR A WELL-BUILT COFFIN?
Peosta

According to casket-business lingo, there are only two kinds of customers: "pre-need" and "need." If you're stumped as to which category you belong, just have a friend or loved one check for a pulse; if there's a heartbeat, then you're a "pre-need" casket shopper, and, if not, well, you really need one, right now. (In fact, a casket, some heavy makeup, and a nice suit of clothes are the only things you'll be needing for a long, long time.)

Pre-need or need, you still want to get the best deal on your eternal digs, and the monks at New Melleray Abbey, located about 12 miles southwest of Dubuque, can help. Whereas most Trappists prefer making jellies and jams to keep their monasteries afloat, the brothers at this towering limestone abbey on a hill selectively harvest trees from their 3,400-acre farm, mill the lumber themselves, and then use it to craft beautifully austere and downright affordable coffins. Their Simple Rectangular Casket model in pine, lined in muslin and padded with straw (no gaudy satin here) sells for $575 (walnut or oak for $895), while their top-of-the-line Premium Rectangular Caskets, in walnut or oak, top out at about $1,400.

Founded by Irish monks in 1849, New Melleray was once home to as many as 150 Trappists, but the population is now down to 38. A Roman Catholic order that originated in La Trappe, France, in the mid-seventeenth century, the Trappists follow the monastic rule of St. Benedict, which consists of contemplative prayer, community worship, and manual labor. For the New Melleray monks, that means rising at 3:15 each morning for prayer, attending church services seven times a day, refraining from eating meat, and working four or five hours each day, either in one of the abbey's fields of soy, corn, alfalfa, or potatoes or turning out simple caskets for both pre-need and in-desperate-need customers.

Forward thinking pre-need patrons have included several bishops and Cardinal Roger Mahoney, Archbishop of Los Angeles; according to the abbey newsletter, one priest even requested that his model be fitted with bookshelves so that he could "enjoy his casket from this side of eternity." (The monks will try to accommodate such special requests as best they can.) "Need" customers make far fewer special requests—none have been made to date, actually—but they also send far fewer letters of appreciation and satisfaction. And we all know it hurts to get stiffed. Consummate salesmen, the monks claim not to prefer one category of customer over the other, and, not surprisingly, the orders keep rolling in from both kinds.

New Melleray Abbey is located south of Peosta at 6500 Melleray Circle, midway between U.S. Highways 151 and 20. They offer simple accommodations and meals for visitors wishing to spend time at the monastery, either as monastic retreatants or simply as guests. (A free-will offering of $30 per day is suggested.) For more information call (563) 588–2319. To order a casket call (888) 433–6934 or visit www.trappist casket.com.

RABBIS WITH ROAD RAGE
Postville

If you happen to be visiting Postville (population 1,600), and find yourself in need of a rabbi, don't despair. With more than three dozen rabbis living and working in town (many of them originally from Brooklyn, New York), Postville has the most rabbis per capita of any place in the country; spin a dreidel in any direction on Main Street and it's likely you'll hit one. And since the rabbis are all adherents of the ultraorthodox Lubavich branch of Hasidism, they aren't very hard to spot, either. They're the ones wearing long beards and side locks, dressed in black coats and black hats. (Notably absent from their clothing are the logos of heavy-farm-equipment manufacturers.)

The rabbis started coming to Postville in 1990, after Aaron Rubashkin, a Lubavitch Hasidim from Brooklyn, converted an abandoned slaughterhouse on the edge of town into a kosher meatpacking plant, complete with its own large menorah on the roof. At first the rabbis (whose job it is to bless and slaughter the animals) commuted back and forth between Brooklyn and Iowa, but eventually they decided to move to Postville with their families, creating a thriving ultraorthodox community in rural Iowa almost overnight.

Along with the rabbis came other newcomers to work the plant, including Mexicans, Guatemalans, Ukrainians, Bosnians, and Czechs. (To give you an idea of just how diverse the workforce is, the slaughterhouse's signage is written in English, Spanish, Yiddish, and Russian.) And while many other small, predominantly white rural towns in Iowa have experienced similar influxes of job-seeking immigrants, Postville's demographic shift attracted significant attention from the national media, in part because of the compelling contrasts between the urban, separatist ultraorthodox Jews and their Midwestern-born and -bred neighbors. (The *New York Times*, the *Chicago Tribune*, and National Public Radio have all done profiles on Postville.) Stories tend to focus on how well the newcomers and locals are getting along.

One bone of contention between longtime Postville residents and ultraorthodox transplants arises on Postville's quiet streets. Deeply ingrained Brooklyn driving techniques, including double-parking, quick U-turns, and tactical tailgating, don't seem to work so well in rural Iowa. But while some slower-paced locals take personal offense to the city driving, others are more philosophical. "You know the saying, 'You can take the boy out of Iowa, but you can't take the Iowa out of the boy'?" asked one local resident, who wished to remain anonymous. "Well, the same applies to folks from the city. You can take the rabbi out of Brooklyn driving, but you can't take the Brooklyn driving out of the rabbi."

Postville is located at the intersections of US 18 and Highway 51. The nearest McDonald's is 25 miles away, but there's a kosher deli, with clocks showing the time all around the world, and an excellent Mexican restaurant downtown.

K E E P   Y O U R   E Y E   O N   T H E   C O R N
P r a i r i e b u r g

In Iowa sitting and watching the corn grow has to be one of the three most popular summer pastimes, just behind eating corn (number 2) and selling corn from the back of a pickup on the side of the road (number 1). For all those people unlucky enough to be living out of "ear-sight" in the summer, though, either because they live in town or happen to be from someplace else, like Boisie or Tulsa or the Bronx, *Iowa Farmer Today,* a Cedar Rapids–based agriculture publication, offers the consolation of CornCam.

For the past three years, CornCam has cast an international spotlight on Jim and Sharon Greif's farm outside of Prairiesburg, offering daily updated images of the corn throughout the spring, summer, and early fall. In the prime growing months of June and July, the Web site can log as many as 40,000 visits from corn lovers all over the country and all over the world. This year, the CornCam has traveled to different but certainly just as green pastures, Brad and Kelly Buchanan's 200-acre farm between Cedar Rapids and Ely. As of this writing, the CornCam shows a pleasant view of tall stalks and arching golden tassels under a nearly cloudless sky of blue. Looking at the picture, it's hard not to feel that all is well on this little patch of earth.

Bob Davis, online director for *Iowa Farmer Today*, doesn't fully understand why the site is so popular, but he thinks it has something to do with the fact that corn registers pretty high on the romantic-vegetable scale. And he has some statistics to back up his theory. When *Iowa Farmer Today* ran a SoybeanCam for two years (we're not joking here), it received 90 percent less traffic than CornCam. "The romance wasn't there as it is for corn," Bob said.

In addition to the CornCam, the *Iowa Farmer Today* Web site offers such links as "A Corn Grower's Guidebook," "A Look at the Kernel," and "The Corn Rootworm Homepage," where you can learn everything you wanted to know, and then some, about the surprisingly complex business of growing corn. You can also e-mail the CornCam Web site and let them know your thoughts or even ask a question. One enthusiastic respondent gave the site a ringing endorsement: "If there's a better site for watching corn grow," he wrote, "I haven't seen it." And another visitor asked a seemingly unanswerable question: "Why is this site so exciting?" As Iowans, we'll naturally assume the question is rhetorical.

To sit and watch the corn grow, go to www.iowafarmer.com.

THE GLORY OF BEING GRUMP
FOR A YEAR
Readlyn

Readlyn posts a warning for all to see on a sign located at the edge of town. READLYN, the sign reads, HOME TO 857 FRIENDLY PEOPLE & ONE OLD GRUMP. Depending on how many grumps you have in your neighborhood (or in your own fam-

Don't say the people of Readlyn didn't warn you.

ily), you may think this quite a remarkable nice person-to-grump ratio, but remember, this is Iowa, where nice people are almost as plentiful as hogs. So who's the old grump, you wonder? Does he live on the wrong side of the tracks in a tiny shack, hurling insults at the merry mailman, the good-natured garbage collector, the pious paperboy? (There's a cartoonish picture of an old codger on the sign, looking not so much grumpy as plain ridiculous, but it's just a picture, not a realistic representation of the town's most surly character.) The sign, however, is a little dishonest on two counts: First, there are actually about ten grumps in town, all over the age of sixty-five, and second, all of them are, according to local Jackie Clemmens, "just the opposite of grumpy."

Back in 1990 the Readlyn's Community Club came up with the idea of electing a town grump every year on the third weekend in June and then holding a Grump Fest in his or her honor. Though you might imagine the qualifications to run for Readlyn grump are quite strict, say, at least ten years of complaining bitterly about present-day youth; twenty years of whining about Iowa's heat waves, tornadoes, floods, and blizzards; and fifteen years of telling stories about how things were so much tougher in the old days, the only two qualifications necessary are (1) the prospective grump must live in Readlyn, and (2) he or she must be sixty-five or older.

With such minimal qualifications it's no wonder the Community Club has managed to select the sorriest bunch of grumps you'll ever meet. As far as we know, not a single one of the so-called grumps has ever cussed a neighborhood dog, turned off the lights and hid on Halloween, or sneered at the thought of a good, old-fashioned hometown parade. On the contrary, each year the town grump marches in the Grump Fest parade, right beside the year's Miss Readlyn, a local high school senior, smiling away in a most ungrumplike fashion. And, each year, Readlyn's grump attends local events and celebrations, marches in county parades, speaks with both the local and national media, and generally serves as an all-too-good-natured Readlyn town ambassador. It's enough to make you long for some good old-fashioned surliness.

If you're really searching for some illwill, Readlyn's annual Grump Fest will be a big disappointment, unless, of course, the beer tent happens to run out of Bud. You won't find any sneering or scowling contests, no head-to-head cuss-offs, no bitter monologue matches featuring soliloquies of the most extreme disapproval. (It does sound fun, though, doesn't it?) Highlights of the real Grump Fest include dancing, not one but two card tournaments (Shuffscup and Pepper), a local talent show where everyone gets a lot of applause, no matter the level of talent, and, of course, a parade featuring the newly coronated grump as well as all past surviving grumps.

Grump Fest is a family affair, where the so-called grumps are nicer than your sweet Aunt Beatrice. So if you go, be sure to be on your best behavior, and don't, we repeat, don't heckle the accordion player at the talent show. If you do, not even the town grumps will think you're funny.

Readlyn is located just south of Highway 3 on County Road V49, midway between Waverly and Oelwein. Grump Fest is held the third weekend of June. For more information call (563) 279–3521.

FORMER FAST-FOOD POSTER BOY FINDS WORK AS UMPIRE
Ryan

It's not easy starting a whole new career in middle age, especially if you happen to be an inflexible 20-foot-tall fiberglass Happy Chef. But with the help of a flatbed truck, about twenty-five strong friends, and a creative auto-body worker, even a statue who's spent his entire life wearing a chef's hat and peddling fast food can find a new home and gainful employment to boot, in this case as an intimidatingly large home plate ump.

Ryan's town park is home to "Iowa's Largest Umpire Statue" (seems like a rather conservative claim, doesn't it?), a former Happy Chef statue from Cedar Rapids who would have been doomed to the large fiberglass statuary dustheap if it hadn't been for the intercession of a local priest, Father Beelner. According to postmaster Leo Wood, one of the men who helped the Happy Chef through his career transition, Father Beelner had long wanted "something distinguished for the park, you know a tank or a jet or something," so when local Pat

McKelly's Cedar Rapids Happy Chef franchise was getting rid of their mascot for a new and improved look, he knew whom to call. "Pat called Father Beelner up and he said, 'If you want something for that ballpark, we're getting rid of our Happy Chef. If you want him, you better come and pick him up.'"

And that's just what Father Beelner and a group of local men did. It took more than twenty of them to lift the at that point not-so-happy chef by hand (the fiberglass groaned and threatened to break under the strain) onto a flatbed truck and prop it up with hay bales for the 30-mile drive to Ryan. "And at that point we didn't even know what we were going to do with it—we just had a Happy Chef," Wood said. But thanks to the ingenuity of a local auto-body worker, the chef became an umpire. "Jerry did a great job: He took his hat off, put his thumb up, gave him a mask . . . and did you see the paint job on him?" And now he stands watch over Ryan's ballpark, his thumb raised in the air, calling everybody out in a genial way altogether uncharacteristic for an ump—with a nice big smile. It seems once a Happy Chef always a Happy Chef, or at least always happy, even when dressed up in an ump's clothes and giving everybody the heave-ho.

Ryan is located on Highway 13, 8 miles south of US 20. The umpire stands at the corner of Ryan Park just behind the baseball diamond.

An Iowa Island Town
Sabula

Accessible only by causeway (from the Iowa side), bridge (from the Illinois side), or boat (from any side), Sabula, from the Latin word *sabulum* meaning "sandy soil," has a decidedly unique flavor in a state with oceans of corn and soy but few natural bodies of water. Just a few feet east of Sabula—only four blocks wide by nine blocks long with a population of 715 ("and that's counting all the dogs," one local said)—flows the main channel of the Mississippi, where barges loaded with coal and grain steam past on their way to St. Louis and points farther south. To the west is a maze of Mississippi backwaters that provide safe haven for blue herons and bald eagles. In winter, commuters crossing the causeway to jobs on the mainland can spot as many as a dozen of the regal birds.

Though the town is surrounded by the Mississippi, it's never been flooded; even during the Great Flood of 1993, the worst flood disaster in U.S. history, the town stayed dry (well, for the most part). Partly as a result of such good fortune, townspeople are, not surprisingly, big fans of the Big Muddy, and on nice summer days it's hard to find someone in town who hasn't been playing on, around, or in the river. Besides birds, beautiful views, peace and quiet, and recreation, the river offers townspeople another benefit. Since the river is their backyard—literally—they don't have to worry about developers bringing in Wal-Mart or building cookie-cutter condominium developments on the edge of town. Now, if they could just do something about the gawkers on the paddle-wheel boat cruises, they could all sunbathe in peace.

Sabula is located on Highway 64, nearly at the Illinois border.

B *ully for* B *ily* C *locks*
Spillville

What's a couple of bachelor Bohemian brother farmers named Bily (pronounced bee-lee) to do during the long, cold northeastern Iowa winters, especially with no wives or children or mothers-in-law to keep them otherwise occupied? Should they (a) take up quilting and sell their handiwork at the county fair; (b) become ham-radio enthusiasts and try to communicate with old acquaintances in their Czech homeland; (c) take up wood carving and painstakingly build some of the biggest and most intricate clocks you've ever seen; (d) take to the bottle, sleep 'til noon, and give up showering; or (e) all of the above?

If you said "e," congratulations, you've got a twisted imagination, but if you wisely answered "c," you're absolutely correct. Brothers Frank and Joseph Bily carved their Bily Clocks every winter for more than forty-five years, in spite of their father's advice that they would be far better off if they spent their time doing something more practical. But what clocks they are! All of the main timepieces are big (8 or 9 feet tall) and elaborately, no, obsessively carved, covered with minutely detailed architectural-style features such as columns, balustrades, and cornices, as well as carved mechanical figures, including saints, apostles, cuckoos, and prominent figures from American history, and, to top it all off, many contain built-in musical chimes. The most elaborate of the clocks took years to build, and each one stands as testament to the skill and dedication of these two brothers who never traveled more than 35 miles from Spillville, as well as to the mind-numbing boredom of Iowa winters early in the twentieth century.

Highlights of the collection, housed in an old brick-front residence in downtown Spillville, include the Apostle Clock (built 1915–1916), which disgorges twelve wooden apostles in a tight-knit group every hour on the hour; the American Pioneer History Clock (1923–1927), which stands 8-feet-tall, weighs more than 500 pounds, and contains fifty-seven panels, each one highlighting an important event in U.S. history; and the Charles Lindbergh Memorial Clock (1928), featuring a carved portrait of Lindbergh in honor of his heroic flight.

The Bily Clock Museum also contains a second floor exhibit honoring the famous Czech composer Antonín Dvořák, who lived in the home with his family during the summer of 1893.

Though it's not known for certain whether Frank and Joseph ever met Dvořák (they were only boys at the time of his visit), they made a clock in his memory, anyway; it's in the shape of a violin with Dvořák's face, bushy beard and all, carved into the body. And why not honor the composer with a clock? After all, the Iowa winters are long, the brothers sure as heck weren't going anywhere, and a couple of carvers probably start to run thin on subjects after forty years of clock making.

The Bily Clock Museum is located at 323 North Main Street, downtown Spillville. From May to October the museum is open daily from 8:00 A.M. to 5:30 P.M. Museum hours vary in March, April, and November, so be sure to call ahead for details: (319) 562–3569. The museum is closed December through February, perhaps in honor of Frank and Joseph's prime clock-building season.

WORLD'S LARGEST FIBERGLASS STRAWBERRY ON A POLE
Strawberry Point

Strawberries aren't very hard to find in this town, at least on signs. Like an egomaniacal parent, the delicate little fruit seems to have given its name to just about every hotel, gift shop, and gathering in town. Just to give a few examples, lest we belabor the point, Strawberry Point is home to the Strawberry Motel, Strawberry Computing, Strawberry Foods, Deli & Bakery, and even Strawberry Leisure Homes.

Actually, we can't blame the strawberry for the proliferation of its moniker in Strawberry Point, but we can blame the Frank Hardy Ad Agency in Dubuque and the tourism-savvy Strawberry Point citizens who dreamt up a 15-foot-tall fiberglass strawberry, complete with glistening yellow seeds, and

A big berry that spread its name all over town.

perched it atop a pole smack dab in front of City Hall. The
Strawberry Point strawberry was manufactured in California—
where else would the world's biggest strawberry come from?—
and then traveled cross-country by train before its installation
on June 20, 1967. Towering 29 feet above Main Street and
hailed as "The Largest Strawberry in the World," the sculpture
immediately became a tourist attraction and helped encourage
the de facto policy of naming everything in town "Strawberry,"
from the motel to the leisure home outfit.

Harry Nolda, owner of Strawberry Point's *Press Journal*,
was one of the people instrumental in bringing the world's
biggest strawberry to town. "We just were sitting around and I
can't remember who came up with the idea. At first we thought
it was kind of crazy, but then we said, 'Why not?' And so we
did it." (Don't most stories, both tragic and comic, begin just
that way?) The Jaycees went door to door collecting money
from townspeople, raising more than $4,300 of the straw-
berry's $6,700 cost. The town chipped in the rest. Though the
group had hoped to deliver the strawberry to City Hall by helicopter ("It would have been something," Harry said, "a 15-foot-
tall strawberry dangling from a helicopter") the cost was
prohibitively high, so it rolled in from Dubuque by truck.

With the name and the big statue, you might imagine
Strawberry Point grows lots of strawberries, but you'd be
wrong. (I was told not to say so, but I'm terrible at keeping
secrets: They don't really grow any!) The name Strawberry
Point came from nineteenth-century soldiers who made frequent stops at a spring outside town where wild strawberries
grew, a spot they called Strawberry Point, on their way
between Dubuque and Fort Atkinson. Now, the town celebrates
its heritage with a Strawberry Days Festival, featuring tractor
pulls, barbershop quartets, and loads of free, yes, that's right,
free strawberries and ice cream.

Only a few months after it was erected, the world's biggest
strawberry was damaged when it was blown from its perch by
a windstorm, but since repair of the hole in its side and re-
installation in June 1968, it's lived a stable, relatively unevent-

ful life. "Lots of people get their pictures taken in front of it, and it's been painted a few times, red and green, of course," Harry said, "but it hasn't fallen since." Here's hoping that it stands tall over Strawberry Point for many years to come, and here's hoping, too, that one day it loosens its death grip on the imaginations of the town's small-business owners. In the meantime if you're looking for a florist, a Laundromat, a baker, or maybe even a mortician in town, just look in the phone book under "strawberry."

Strawberry Point is located due east of Oelwein, at the intersection of Highways 3 and 13. The world's largest strawberry can be found downtown, right in front of City Hall. The Strawberry Days Festival is held each summer in the middle of June, with free strawberries and ice cream served at the firehouse on Sunday. Call Fay Falck at (563) 933–4370 for more information.

MORE THAN 1,000 CLOCKS THAT (THANKFULLY) DON'T CHIME ALL AT ONCE
Waukon

Sweeney's House of Clocks & Museum is one of those Iowa wayside treasure troves that doesn't have regular hours, which makes a visit there all the more personal and all the more wonderfully surreal. In order to get into the building, really just an oversized aluminum storage barn, you have to stop into Sweeney's Village Farm and Home Store, the place with the 20-foot-tall fiberglass steer out front, pawing the ground right beside the 30-foot cowboy, who looks suspiciously like a muffler man who's been given a ten-gallon hat and a new paint job. Ask about the museum at the counter, and a member of one generation or another of the Sweeney family will proba-

Does anyone have the time . . . to wind all these clocks?

bly call Norris Shefelbrin to see if he can come down from the retirement community up the hill to open the place up. "They serve dinner to the residents about eleven, eleven-thirty, so he may need to make it quick," one of the Sweeneys told us. The pressure was on.

Norris met us at the door a few minutes later, shook our hands, unlocked the doors, collected his four bucks and then told us that the oldest clock of the 1,000 or so in the place, made in 1692, was the small black table clock in the back corner. And then, without further ado, he let us know his work was done. "That's about all I can tell you. I just do this as a pastime. And I don't go around and wind 'em all, either." With that short but refreshingly frank introduction, he turned us loose to marvel at the rows and rows of mantel clocks, kitchen clocks, grandfather clocks, and so on, as well as the oddball assortment of antiques, memorabilia, and artifacts.

Sweeney's House of Clocks and Museum is actually two collections combined into one. The first is Ray Tlougan's mammoth collection of clocks, begun in the summer of 1960 when Ray rescued a grandfather clock from a garbage truck and expanded continuously for the next seventeen years. Restoring the grandfather prompted him to begin snapping up other damaged clocks, replacing their clockworks, and repairing their cabinetry. Soon he was not only restoring clocks but carving his own (more than 75 percent of the collection Ray made himself), using only a cheap jigsaw and a pocket knife. In a stroke of marketing genius, Ray decided to take advantage of the clock tourist traffic by showcasing the whole lot in Spillville, right across the street from the Bily Clock museum. Though most of the collection is composed of pretty standard-looking clocks, there are a few standouts, including a French onyx clock made for an Egyptian ruler in 1878 and a 10-foot-tall Belgian grandfather clock made in the early 1700s, featuring a carved stag's head with a full set of antlers at the very top.

The second part of the collection is Ray Sweeney's museum, an eclectic assortment of old stuff, most of which hails from Allamakee County, including a two-cylinder, chain-driven 1907 Sears & Roebuck automobile (in working condition), a chair whose arms, feet, and back are all made of animal horns, two seated, life-sized Indians flanked by two mannequins dressed in World War II–era military uniforms, various and sundry political buttons, old china, and a miniature reproduction of Festina's "Littlest Church." In addition to the fascinating sundries inside, Ray Sweeney also dragged six railroad cars, a very small chapel, his boyhood schoolhouse (really), and a restored settler's cabin up the hill, which, needless to say, produces an interesting architectural landscape effect, a mixture of abandoned railroad yard and abandoned historic village.

Norris wasn't quite being honest when he claimed he didn't know anything else about the museum; he ending up pointing out a number of his favorite items, which included the old jalopy and the miniature Festina chapel, and then chewed the fat with us about nothing in particular. And he didn't even rush us the least bit, even though his dinner was surely getting cold.

Sweeney's House of Clocks and Museum is located a half mile south of Waukon on Highways 9 and 76. Open by appointment. Stop by Sweeney's Village Farm and Home Store or call (563) 568–4577.

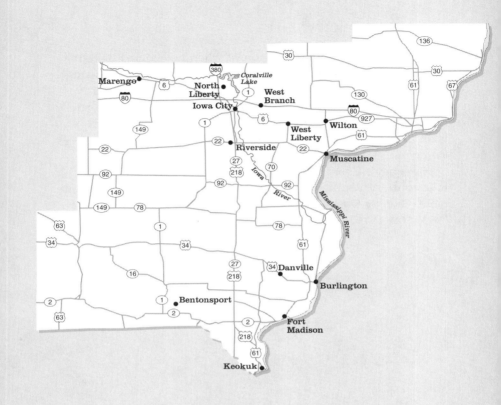

SOUTHEAST

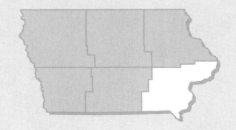

SOUTHEAST

A TUB FOR THE EXHIBITIONIST IN YOU
Bentonsport

Across between a living museum and a town, Bentonsport is the most beautiful of the Van Buren County river towns, a tiny place of about fifty residents that was once a bustling steamboat port and home to more than 1,500. Many of the buildings, most of which date from the mid-nineteenth century, have white placards out front listing the date of construction and a brief history. Highlights include Bill and Betty Printy's blacksmith shop and gift store, the brick Federal-style Greef's General Store, the Vernon School House (just across the Des Moines River), now an art gallery and home of artist-in-residence Wendell Mohr, and the Mason House Inn.

Built in 1846 by Mormon workmen who dropped out of the westward trek to Utah (temporarily, say the brochures, but we're not so easily convinced), the Mason House Inn is the oldest steamboat hotel in continuous use along the Des Moines River. Now owned and operated by Chuck and Joy Hanson as a bed-and-breakfast, the Mason House boasts a cookie jar in every room (each more or less full depending on the willpower of the occupants) and is chock-full of antiques that were original to the hotel, including beds, dressers, an 1880 Buck's woodstove, an indoor well pump, and a Murphy tub.

Modesty is a virtue, but cleanliness is
next to Godliness.

Don't know what a Murphy tub is? Located in the Keeping Room at the back of the inn—the Keeping Room served as the family's living quarters—the Mason House Murphy tub is a fold-down, copper-lined tub that stows away in a cabinet in the wall when not in use. The only one of its kind in Iowa, the tub is in the middle of the room, right next to the fireplace so that water could be heated and added to the tub at will. Depending on your level of comfort with your body and your inclinations toward exhibitionism, though, the Murphy tub is either a dream come true or your worst nightmare. There's no screen around the tub, and the chance of a little privacy in the Keeping Room, where the owners still do much of their living, is slim to none. If you do brave the waters, though, at least there'll be plenty of help around should you need someone to scrub your back.

Mason House Inn is located at 21982 Hawk Drive, Bentonsport. For more information and reservations, call (319) 592–3133.

NO LIGHTS, NO ADMISSION FEE
Burlington

Starr Cave Park and Preserve is one of the few nature parks in the state that requires batteries—for your flashlight, of course. And though park operators won't kick you out for wearing your L.L. Bean– or Eddie Bauer–best, park operators recommend more casual dress. In other words, wear things you don't mind getting very, very muddy. (They also note that if someone calls you a spelunker, take no offense; it's not an insult.)

Composed of three caves, 200 acres of woodland and restored prairie, and several miles of nature trails, Starr Cave Park is what every Mississippi River town deserves but few have—a patch of woods and a natural cave to explore, without lights or guides or concrete paths, that would make even Tom Sawyer a little jealous. Of the three caves on the preserve, only Starr Cave was made by Mother Nature (the other two were created by Mother Dynamite), and only Starr Cave will get you truly muddy. Carved out of limestone cliffs along Flint Creek, the narrow cave is closed to the public between October 1 and April 1 to protect hibernating bats. During summer, however, you and the bats are allowed to fraternize, though the bats ask that you be respectful of the fact that they all work the graveyard shift.

Starr Cave Park and Preserve is open daily 6:00 A.M. to
10:30 P.M. and is off U.S. Highway 61. Turn east on Sunnyside
Road, go ½ mile and turn north onto Irish Ridge Road. Go ½
mile and the entrance will be on the left. Follow the brown
signs with white arrowheads. Starr Cave is open only April 1
to October 1.

TWIST AND TURN ON SNAKE ALLEY
Burlington

It's quite possible that extremely windy, bumpy streets aren't
high on your list of holiday destinations. You may not be a
fan of such streets, or, more likely (because, after all, who doesn't
love a rough and crooked road?), you may be lucky enough to
have numerous pot-hole-dotted streets in your own county to
choose from whenever you need to satisfy a craving. But even if
your local road crews seem to have taken the last three years off
and you've got many of your own hometown favorites, you'll
still want to visit Burlington's Snake Alley, just about the
crookedest and bumpiest street you're likely ever to find.

Reminiscent of San Francisco's Lombard Street and hailed
by *Ripley's Believe It or Not* as the crookedest street in the
world, Snake Alley is composed of two quarter turns and five
half turns carved into a steep hillside overlooking Burlington's
downtown shopping district. Engineers and contractors built
the street in 1894, laying each paving brick on its side and at a
downward angle to provide horses better footing (and, hope-
fully, more horsepower) as they traversed the steep grade. (Legend has it that the Burlington Fire Department used Snake
Alley to test the mettle of its horses.) The end result is a very
steep street that looks like a coiled snake wearing a brick-
ribbed sweater, a crooked and bumpy street-lover's dream.

No longer open to street traffic except by permission, Snake Alley makes for a lovely winding walk 58 vertical feet down Heritage Hill to the shopping district below. Bordered by rough-cut granite walls and sculpted patches of fairway-green grass, the street is truly a lovely piece of landscape architecture, winding its way beside a large red-brick church, the First United Church of Christ, and a number of well preserved nineteenth-century homes.

All the tourist guidebooks celebrate this beautiful landmark of the Queen City, as Burlington used to be known, but the rest of the city is quite lovely, too, perched as it is on hills overlooking the Mississippi. If you explore some of the smoother streets in town, you'll find many stately older homes, brick and granite structures with elaborately carved and ornately painted wooden fascias. Burlington is second only to Dubuque in terms of natural beauty—a view of the mighty river is never more than a few blocks away. But if you're anything like us, when it comes to sight-seeing, nothing quite compares to some really good curves and bumps in the road.

Snake Alley runs between Washington and Columbia Streets on Sixth Street in downtown Burlington.

S *LEEP* $I N$ *A* B *ARN;* B *ATHE* $I N$ *A* H *OT* T *UB*
Danville

Your mother never imagined a place like this when she asked you (and she most certainly asked you this, even if you don't remember it) "What, do you live in a barn?!" Of course, the question was rhetorical. She didn't expect an answer. Your mother knew quite well where you lived, and how you lived, and what state of chaos your room was in (and maybe

Here's your chance to sleep in the barn.

even still does). Even so, she couldn't understand why, every time you left the house, you neglected to close the door. Thus, the barn question. Barns have doors. And presumably, moms wouldn't care if said doors were left open. At least that was the subtle message mom was sending, if you think about it.

Mom probably never guessed that you might some day spend money to live, for a night or two, in a barn, but that's just what you can do at the Secret Garden in Danville. Owners Kristen and Ryan Gourley renovated the barn of their 1846 Sesquicentennial farm, installed a hot tub and a comfy double bed in the hayloft, along with other amenities, and created the perfect romantic hideaway. But the best part of the barn bed-and-breakfast is that the rear doors open up onto a private meadow, so you can shove the barn doors wide open and leave them that way, all day and night, enjoy the fresh air, and still have privacy.

The name the Secret Garden refers to a small sitting place just across the pond, as well as to the fact that Kristen and Ryan, both expert botanists, also run a flower farm on the eighteen-acre grounds. And the scent of all those flowers, both fresh and dried, is yet another reason to indulge the kid in you and throw the barn doors wide open. Could it be that our moms were really onto something with the barn idea?

The Secret Garden is located at 10182 Danville Road, at the intersection with County Road X31. For more information or reservations, call (319) 392–8288 or e-mail Ryan at ryan@the-secret-garden.net.

C O N E S   A N D   K I D S   O N   T H E   O U T S I D E
F o r t   M a d i s o n

If a 20-foot concrete soft-serve ice-cream cone and a concrete giraffe don't make a strange enough sight for you, then try tossing a 50-foot-tall guard tower into the mix and you'll begin to get a sense of what a surreal place the ice-cream stand at the northwestern corner of the Fort Madison State Penitentiary truly is. The gothic guard tower and the almost laughably huge, depressing and dispiriting prison walls (made of drab gray stone, more than 35 feet tall in places, supported by giant buttresses) are mere yards away from this soft-serve ice-cream stand, 18-hole miniature golf course, and batting cage. (Batters face the prison walls—Do they imagine they are knocking a home run right into the "pen"?)

Step right up (under surveillance, of course) and order a cone from an apple-cheeked youngster. Lick your cone, watch the kids frolic on the Astroturf, and try not to be distracted by the coils of concertina wire over your left shoulder or the shadows at your feet cast by the looming prison walls. And not just any prison

An ice-cream stand with a strong anticrime message.
Photo: Catherine Cole

walls. The Fort Madison State Penitentiary, a maximum-security prison, was first built in 1839, before Iowa even attained statehood. There've been many additions and renovations since then, of course, but the original cellblock is still in use, and three of the prison houses are on the National Register of Historic Places. (Just as a side note, we suggest you avoid historic prisons should you ever decide to get incarcerated. Historic homes, good; historic prisons, bad.)

The penitentiary's overall effect makes Alcatraz look like Fantasy Island, but it's probably the only maximum-security prison in the country, and perhaps in the world, where you can bring the kids to the prison walls and make a night of it, putting for par, swinging for the bleachers (or the guard-house), and finishing it all off with an ice-cream sundae, two cherries on top. Could Midwestern leisure get any weirder?

The Fort Madison State Penitentiary and the ice-cream stand are on US 61, just northwest of downtown Fort Madison.

A CURSED STATUE WITH A PRUDISH STREAK
Iowa City

I f it weren't for all those graves, you might confuse Iowa City's Oakland Cemetery for a well-designed park. The land rises and falls to form gentle knolls and valleys; mature maple, oak, and cedar line the narrow asphalt roads, and the lawns are brilliantly green and impeccably groomed three seasons of the year. The cemetery's eastern edge abuts Hickory Hill Park, and dog walkers and joggers are a common sight among the headstones as they make their way to sniff and/or pound the park's trails.

Doesn't sound very spooky, does it? But wait: We forgot to mention that in the middle of the cemetery is an infamous cursed statue, a towering, 9-foot-tall black angel, her massive bronze wings folded earthward, her heavy head hanging low, looking so downtrodden and weary you'll want to help her off her cold pedestal and put her to rest.

Don't offer her your sympathy so fast, though. Among the many legends surrounding the so-called Black Angel is that any girl kissed near her in the moonlight will die within six months. Another myth has it that anyone who kisses the statue dies instantly. Yet another says that the Black Angel turned black (it's original color was bronze) and continues to have such ill effects on people because of a wife's infidelity.

An angel with a heavy heart—and a possible
case of osteoporosis.

Come to think of it, almost every legend surrounding her has something to do with kissing and death, in that order. Whoever and whatever the Black Angel is, one thing is sure: She's reputed to be a strong, and strong-handed, advocate of abstinence, at least in her cemetery.

One true story concerning the Black Angel is that she was commissioned by a Czech midwife, Teresa Dolezal Feldevert, who emigrated to Iowa City in the late nineteenth century, to mark the graves of her second husband, Nicholas Feldevert, and her son, Eddie Dolezal, who died at age eighteen. When Teresa died in 1924, she too was buried in the shadow of the Black Angel's massive wings. One of the many peculiarities of the tomb, however, is that although Mrs. Feldevert's year of birth is engraved on the base, her year of death is absent, as if she were still alive. Even more unusual is the Black Angel's position: whereas most angels on tombstones are depicted with heads and wings uplifted to symbolize the soul's ascent into heaven, the Black Angel, shoulders slumped, wings folded downward, looks like Atlas carrying the weight of the world on her back.

Perhaps the least mysterious aspect of the legend surrounding the Black Angel is why she turned black. (Curious citizens have chipped away at some of the black in places, trying to catch a glimpse of what's underneath.) The answer: good old-fashioned oxidation of the bronze in which she was cast. But your guess is as good as ours as to why the Black Angel is so dead-set against a little kissing.

At the corner of Brown and Governor Streets, Oakland Cemetery is open from 7:00 A.M. to 9:00 P.M., seven days a week. After you enter the main gate, follow the asphalt path east until you see the Black Angel.

LONG JOURNEY WITH NO BAGGAGE CHECK
Iowa City

Just prior to the Civil War, Iowa City was the soon-to-be-completed transcontinental railroad's western terminus. If you traveled any farther west, across the prairie and onward to the Great Plains, to seek land, fortune, and/or adventure, you couldn't do it in cushioned comfort at an even 40 or 50 miles per hour. Instead, you went by horse and wagon (preferably covered), and the ride was bumpier, longer, hotter, and more perilous than we can probably imagine.

Or, if you were Mormon, you proved your mettle by avoiding conveyances entirely and traveling by foot, pulling all your worldly possessions behind you in a homemade handcart. In May 1856 the first of a group of 1,900 British and Scandinavian members of the Church of Jesus Christ of Latter-Day Saints, or Mormons, arrived in Iowa City and set up camp on the western edge of town. Their ultimate goal was Salt Lake City, Utah, more than 1,300 miles away, but they had a few minor challenges to overcome before they got there, not the least of which was that they were too poor to buy horses, wagons, or even handcarts.

When the Mormon leader, Brigham Young, heard of their plight, he was reported to have said, "Let them come on foot, with handcarts or wheelbarrows, let them gird up their loins and walk through." And that's exactly what they did, making their own handcarts, loading up their possessions (each person was allowed seventeen pounds of belongings), and walking from Iowa City to Utah in five separate handcart companies that averaged about 15 miles a day throughout the spring, summer, and early fall.

Mormon Handcart Park, an unassuming gem of a park tucked behind university athletic fields off Mormon Trek Boulevard, marks the spot of the original encampment, which, the placards tell us, looks much the same as it did when the Mormons were preparing for their journey. Mormon Handcart Park is located at the end of Hawkeye Court Road, off Mormon Trek Boulevard. For more information call (319) 335–1049.

Peace and Quiet in a Padded Room
Iowa City

Researchers say there are only a few places left in the world free from the noise of humankind's almost infinite variety of whirring, whining, and chugging machines. What's that, you didn't hear us? Before your cellphone rang, or the fax beeped, or that twenty-ton semi downshifted on the interstate, we were talking about how noisy our modern world has become. Silence is now such a rare and precious commodity, it can no longer be called merely golden; it must have graduated to platinum long ago, maybe sometime in the seventies, only no one bothered to fill us all in.

The Wendell Johnson Hearing Center's Anechoic Chamber (*anechoic* means "without echo") provides architectural evidence that people will go to almost any lengths to find some peace and quiet. Used most commonly to test hearing, the 27,000 cubic-foot-chamber was designed and built with one goal in mind: to minimize external noise and internal sound reflection to create as silent a room as possible. The engineers covered its thick walls in 36-inch sound-absorbent wedges and then made sure the basketball-court-sized chamber's only contact with floor, walls, and ceiling (and the outside world) was through a series of structural springs. The end result is a room so quiet that you'll imagine you can hear your own blood coursing through your veins and, after a few minutes more, the whine of your central nervous system. If you hear more than that, you might be hallucinating, but fear not, the University Psychiatry Department is only a few feet away.

The chamber is located at 110 Hawkins Drive and is open weekdays from 8:00 A.M. to 5:00 P.M. For more information call (319) 335–8736. Though the chamber is not open to the public, you might be allowed to look if you ask politely; call before you go to ask permission.

OLD-FASHIONED TAXIDERMY
Iowa City

Where can you go to find a 13-foot giant sloth wearing a Santa suit, a 46-foot right-whale skeleton, and a hummingbird egg about as big as your thumbnail? If you're in Iowa City, the answer is MacBride Hall, located a few steps northeast of the Old Capitol on the University's Pentacrest and home to the University of Iowa's Museum of Natural History. The museum's oldest galleries, Mammal Hall and the William and Eleanor Hageboeck Hall of Birds, both located on the third floor, have been in existence since 1858, making the Museum of Natural History the oldest university museum west of the Mississippi.

But if mere old age isn't enough to tempt you, then consider this: Over a century ago a museum of natural history meant one thing: lots and lots of exotic dead animals. Mammal Hall contains hundreds of them, including a panther, a zebra, a rhino (complete with dried mud on his back), a wolf, a wombat, and an aardvark, down the great chain of being to lowly squirrels and mice (at least a dozen different varieties of each), all

A sloth who knows how to party.

killed and then stuffed for the sole purpose of being displayed in dioramas of the Serengeti or the Arctic or the less exotic Iowa countryside. Don't miss standing directly under the massive ribs of the right whale suspended from the hall's ceiling; the skeleton alone weighs in at 4,000 pounds.

More than a thousand stuffed birds fill Bird Hall, including a remarkable glass case of more than one hundred different bird eggs, a peacock in mesmerizing tail spread, and a nearly 360-degree diorama, or cyclorama, of a South Pacific island, complete with a gaggle or two of stuffed native birds in the foreground. The project took an early-twentieth-century University-sponsored expedition of a professor, two students, and a professional background artist almost four years to complete. There are a few attempts to make the museum a little more twenty-first century, including a large diorama (under construction as of publication) detailing the dramatic ecological changes humans have wrought in Iowa, the state where, the caption says, "people have altered the landscape more dramatically than any other. . . ." But for the most part, the third-floor halls have remained pure nineteenth century, and it's enough to make a visitor reel from science culture shock.

The museum's main exhibit space is on MacBride's first floor, Iowa Hall, a gallery that explores 500 million years of Iowa's ecology, geology, and cultural history. Here you'll find what museum coordinator David Brenzel lovingly refers to as "our star," a towering giant sloth, bizarre snout in the air, massive claws reaching for the foliage on some tree from the Ice Age. (If you come at the right time, you might find him dressed for the season as a pilgrim or even jolly old St. Nick.)

MacBride Hall is located downtown on the University of Iowa's Pentacrest, at the corner of Iowa Avenue and Clinton Street. Hours of operation are Monday through Saturday from 9:30 A.M. to 4:30 P.M. and Sunday from 12:30 to 4:30 P.M. For more information call (319) 335–0480.

A SHOPPER'S ORGY
Iowa City

If you're looking to buy a one-hundred-year-old deer rifle, a silver mercury dime from the 1930s, and a loaf of bread from a Mennonite farmer named Cephis Yoder, there's only one place for you to go: Iowa City's Sharpless Auction. Held every Wednesday night from 5:30 P.M. to around 9:00 P.M., it's the state's biggest indoor auction, averaging 400 bidders in winter and more than twice that in the peak summer months, when the better merchandise arrives.

And, oh, the merchandise. Fresh-from-the-old-farmhouse goods run the gamut from green vinyl couches to covet-fit-inducing antique oak dressers, from headless Barbie dolls to grandma's heirloom china. Everything you'd ever dream of finding in an old attic, garage, bedroom, kitchen, or barn is here, spread out on tables and along the walls in no particular order, at least none that we could decipher.

Grab your auction number, stand by your find, and size up the competition as you wait for the auctioneer on the podium to move the bidding from the front to the back of the room. Remember, only novices raise a number early, since the auctioneer tends to start the bid laughably high. (Why does he talk so fast, and why does that high-speed, tongue-twirling drone make us so eager to buy?) And be sure to keep your Midwestern hospitality in check: One errant wave to a neighbor at the Mennonite baked-goods table might mean you'll go home with a musty feather boa you'll never, ever wear.

Sharpless Auctions is on Interstate 80, just off exit 249, the first exit east of Iowa City. Auctions take place on Wednesday nights and begin at 5:30 P.M.

G O U R M E T   D I N I N G   I N   K E O K U K ?
K e o k u k

It's a gastronomical falsehood that we Iowans stick to pork and potatoes at the dinner table. Some of us occasionally dabble in fish, too, though usually in the form of Friday-night fish sticks. But here, in a lovingly restored Italianate villa–style home in this old river city, we find a five-star restaurant and cooking school run by a woman hailed by numerous food-magazine editors as one of the region's finest chefs.

Though the following names may not mean a whole lot to those of us whose teeth buzz through sweet corn faster than combines, Liz Clark received a diploma from La Varenne in Paris, studied at Moulin de Mougin with Roger Verge, and received further education at the Oriental in Bangkok. Translation for the nonfoodies out there: Liz studied at some of the finest cooking schools and with some of the most accomplished chefs in the world and not only knows the difference between foie gras and pâté, but can whip up some impressive examples of both. But lest we give the wrong impression of Liz as a snobbish gourmet, she taught her most recent class at the local Hy-Vee grocery on how to talk to your butcher when searching for the best cuts of meat. (Could there be more to it than making eye contact, smiling, complimenting him on his new white apron, and listening carefully to his concerns?) "We do casseroles, too," she says of her restaurant in a matter-of-fact tone. (What about Jell-O molds, we wonder?) After all, she says, though she was trained in France, she's Iowa born and raised.

On Saturdays and Sundays Liz offers cooking classes on everything from tapas to chocolate desserts in the impressive home she has spent the last three decades restoring. Though her cooking classes are most often group affairs, her seven-course dinners are decidedly intimate: She takes only one reservation per evening, and during the busy season she's booked weeks and sometimes months in advance. You can let her know of any food allergies and favorites and she'll accommodate, but she reserves the right to set the menu as she sees fit. "I'm a bit of a nut when it comes to using the best and the freshest in-season ingredients," she says. "If I go to the farmer's market that day, and there's a wonderfully fresh ingredient that'll only be around for a few weeks, then by gum I'm gonna use it." And by gum, with a chef like Liz, five-star French cuisine feels downright homegrown.

Liz is located at 116 Concert Street. For information about meals and/or cooking classes, call (319) 524–4716.

HUGE DAM, LOTS OF SILT
Keokuk

Way back in 1913, when this wonder of the world was built on the Mississippi between Keokuk and Hamilton, Illinois, the Keokuk hydroelectric plant was supposed to provide nearly free electricity and create a large lake upstream. The largest hydroelectric dam in the world at the time of its completion, the Keokuk plant is an impressively large wall of earth, rock, and concrete that measures almost a mile wide and more than ten stories high in places. Such a massive dam did

They don't call it the Big Muddy for nothing.

create a large lake (about 50 square miles large), but the lake silted up, as did the generators, and the whole thing served as a monument to the perils of boosterism and wishful thinking.

At present it still generates electricity and provides a lock, the largest on the Mississippi, for barges and big boats. The plant used to offer daily tours, but they were discontinued when it changed hands a few years ago, so you'll have to take in the operation from the riverbank. The Keokuk Power Plant is not just a lock and dam, it's a symbol of hope in progress, of faith in science and industry, of the triumph of human technology over the forces of nature. We'd just hate to be the guy who has to scrape the muck from the turbines to keep the whole show going.

The dam is located at 523 North Water Street.

THE MOTEL THAT TIME FORGOT
Marengo

Just outside Marengo on Highway 6 is Sudbury Court Motel, a perfectly preserved 1940s row-style motel, complete with sturdy-looking gray stone walls, posters of mountains and forests just above the headboards, and a recently reconditioned Art Deco neon sign as brilliantly blue as the Midwestern sky. If you're interested in the latest renovations, the owner, Tricia Hocamp, might pull her Sudbury Court photo album from behind the front desk and show you what she, her husband Tony, and a number of fairly photogenic subcontractors have been up to. For starters they moved the nineteenth century "boarding house," (the original Sudbury motel that locals claim was a brothel) down the street on a flatbed, put awnings over the motel doors to protect guests from rain, and planted a tree farm with more than 1,000 trees.

With its pristine rooms, staid gray walls, and beautifully glowing neon sign, a stay at the Sudbury Court is like traveling back to an older America, circa 1949. Step out the red door of room 5, lean against the stones, watch the sun set over the fields of whispering corn, and it isn't very hard to imagine yourself a traveling salesman dreaming of all those postwar families beyond the stalks just itching to buy, buy, buy.

Sudbury Court Motel is located at 2211 U.S. Highway 6, just outside of Marengo. For more information or reservations, call (319) 642–5411.

The AARP Meets the Ritz
Muscatine

What do you get when you cross the Ritz with senior-citizen housing? We know that sounds like the lead line to a joke (the punch line: Five-Star Bingo), but it's also a perfect description of the Hotel Muscatine, a grand Mississippi hotel in downtown Muscatine that's been converted into apartments for the elderly. Opened in 1915, this was Muscatine's version of the Blackhawk in Davenport or the Blackstone in Chicago, a luxurious hotel for the well-to-do and upwardly mobile classes.

In the 1920s, with button-baron families still in town, slot machines lined the ballroom walls, and dancers whirled to the sounds of a live orchestra. The hotel's grandeur faded some with time, but major restoration undertaken in the early 1980s, including extensive repair of oak pillars and banisters in the lobby, helped restore the building's original luster.

Even though the Hotel Muscatine now comprises private apartments for seniors, you can still walk around the lobby, admire all that Italian marble and hand-carved oak, and imagine the place bustling with well-heeled patrons. So what do you get when you cross a fancy hotel with senior-citizen housing? Gourmands who request the early-bird special? No, just the Hotel Muscatine.

The Hotel Muscatine can be found downtown on US 61, right on the riverfront.

BUTTONS OF YESTERYEAR
Muscatine

Around the turn of the century, Muscatine produced more than 1.5 billion buttons per year, nearly 40 percent of the world's annual supply. At the height of production, more than forty-three factories stamped button blanks out of mussel shells dragged from the Mississippi River, which were then finished in home workshops scattered throughout the city. Townspeople produced so many buttons that in a moment of uncharacteristic Iowa boastfulness, Muscatine dubbed itself the "Pearl Button Capital of the World."

The Pearl Button Museum is a downtown Muscatine storefront devoted to the history of what was once the area's biggest industry. You'll learn about the inventive and enterprising German immigrant John Boepple, who discovered that mussels from the Mississippi worked just as well as the more costly animal horns traditionally used for button making. Thanks to his ingenuity, between 1885 and 1910, Mississippi river mussels were bivalvular gold for communities all the way from Marquette south to Keokuk, providing Boepple and others with the raw material needed to keep half the world's shirts and dresses fastened for another year. The museum features beautiful old photographs, loads of buttons, and probably more details than you might care to know about the process of making buttons out of shells at the turn of the century.

Plastic spelled the end of Muscatine's button-making brag-gadocio, and a bustling industry vanished almost overnight. If you don't believe a whole museum could be dedicated to such a mundane but serviceable object as the button and still be more interesting than yard work, the Pearl Button Museum will prove you wrong.

The Pearl Button Museum is located right downtown, at 117 West Second Street. For more information call (563) 263–1052 or visit www.pearlbutton.org. Admission is free, but donations are gladly accepted. The museum is open Tuesday through Saturday from noon to 4:00 P.M. or by appointment.

CAUGHT BETWEEN THE MOON AND IOWA
Muscatine

Want an exotic vacation but don't quite have the cash to get to Cairo? A close or distant second, depending on your affinity for kitsch, might be a stay at the Econo Lodge Fanta-suite Motel, located on the northern edge of Muscatine, a delight-ful Mississippi River town about 27 miles south of the Quad Cities. It's lowbrow luxury, of course, but we Iowans tend to be a practical people. After all, why spend a mattress full of money on pricey hotels, fancy food, and tours when you can stick close to home and just pretend you've gone somewhere instead?

Indulge yourself in any one of a number of fantasies, depending on your mood. Feeling a little intergalactic? Then slip into the moon-crater whirlpool in the Space Odyssey Suite. Or, if it suits your fantasy, raise the dead in the Pharaoh's Chamber. For the weary traveler the Arabian Nights Suite offers desert-oasis accommodations, not to mention an octago-nal bed. All suites feature whirlpool baths and romantic extras, in a mirrors-on-the-ceiling sort of way.

That charge you hear leveled against so many hotel rooms—that they all look the same, whether you're in Des Moines or Saigon—certainly doesn't apply here. If you're the type who feels most comfortable with the mundane, though, the motel also offers everyday rooms at a more modest price. (It's never cheap to indulge your fantasies, even close to home.) If you play it safe, be sure to take the tour of rooms offered each day at 3:00 P.M., so that you can at least get a glance at the spaceship bed and see how the Jetson-set lives.

The hotel is located at 2402 Park Avenue on the northern edge of town. For more information or reservations, call (563) 264–3337.

NOT YOUR UNCLE LENNY'S PHOTO ALBUM
Muscatine

What if one hundred years from now someone found your personal photos carefully preserved in a long-abandoned attic? Would your photo albums be about as interesting to future Americans as Uncle Lenny's slide show from his trip to Disneyland? Or would they be so impressed with the way you had captured late twentieth- and early twenty-first-century life on film that they'd take the whole collection, name it after you, and preserve it in your local library as a historical artifact and cultural resource for generations to come?

If the answer is the former, then try not to feel too envious of Oscar Grossheim, because after discovering his sizable photo collection—he took more than 55,000 pictures between 1887 and 1954—they made it available for your perusal at the Musser Public library in downtown Muscatine. The pictures, printed from perfectly preserved photographic plates, offer a staggeringly detailed record of life in a small Midwestern town at the turn of the century. Every house, every store window, every civic group, every prominent citizen and his or her family, every local parade, even every nearby train wreck—all are things Grossheim found fascinating enough to photograph, and photograph well.

Not only can you browse through the many binders of prints, you can order your own copies for a measly $5.00 a photo, as long as you don't intend to use or sell the print professionally. Spend an afternoon poring over the archives, pick out the ones you like, and a library volunteer will print your negatives and send them to you in the mail. It may take a little while, but it's well worth the wait. And Mr. Grossheim's collection just might inspire you to start photographing your local mayor, or the bank president who lives down the street, or even the postman, all for posterity, of course, and a special spot in your local library in the year 2145. If they happen to ask what you think you're doing, just don't tell them we put you up to it.

The Musser Public Library is located at 304 Iowa Avenue in downtown Muscatine. The library is open Monday through Thursday 10:00 A.M. to 9:00 P.M., Friday 10:00 A.M. to 6:00 P.M., and Saturday 10:00 A.M. to 4:00 P.M. For more information call (563) 263–3472.

RADIO DEMAGOGUE AND QUACK NORMAN BAKER
Muscatine

Most towns memorialize only their most admirable and honorable citizens: war heroes, suffragists, civic leaders. Muscatine boldly bucked this trend and decided to immortalize a homegrown quack instead. No doubt, Norman Baker is one

man many Muscatinians would sooner forget, but for some reason there's a small plaque (or back of a plaque) dedicated to
him and his radio station just up the hill from town.

The front of the plaque features a quote from Mark Twain,
who used to spend summers in Iowa, about how beautiful the
sunsets are in Muscatine, whereas the back notes that the site
was the location of Muscatine's first radio station, KTNT, or
Know The Naked Truth, founded by Norman Baker himself. We
all know who Mark Twain was (white hair, handlebar mus-
tache, a satirical streak in him a mile wide), and those of us
who've been to Muscatine know how pretty the sunsets are, but
who in the world was Norman Baker? Turns out Baker's pair-
ing with Twain is more apt than you might think, because he
just so happened to be Muscatine's most infamous conman, a
reputed charlatan who could have easily stepped from the
pages of one of Twain's dark, comic tales.

Norman Baker decided one day that Muscatine needed its
own radio station and that he was just the man to build it. By
running huge copper cables from his homemade transmitter all
the way down the hill to the Mississippi, Baker turned the Big
Muddy into a giant reflector for his signal, located at 1170 on
the AM dial. In doing so he paid nominal heed to FCC-imposed
broadcasting power limits; some old-timers claim that on winter nights KTNT could be heard halfway across the country.

In many ways it was a typical AM station of the day, with
programming that featured chamber concerts, inspirational
readings, and Baker's daily rants. But Baker also spent a fair
amount of airtime advertising a miracle cure for cancer, available only at the "hospital" he himself headed. Because there
were few treatments for cancer in those days, desperate and
dying patients were willing to try anything, including a stay
at Baker's hospital, where the morning lines for admission
sometimes stretched around the block. How successful were the
treatments? Some say the number of bodies taken away by
hearse after dark each night came close to the number of daily
admits. The radio station kept new customers coming from

near and far, and to this day no one knows how much money Baker made off the enterprise.

It wasn't long before both the American Medical Association and the FCC began pressuring Baker to close up shop. Finally, in 1931 the FCC pulled his license, putting an end to both KTNT and Baker's "medical career" in Iowa. Undeterred, Baker repaired to Hot Springs, Arkansas, bought an old hotel, and went back into the radio and cancer-treatment businesses. Later, when he was asked to leave Arkansas, he moved just across the Mexican border and set up a 100,000 watt station that, if conditions were right, could be heard clearly back in Muscatine.

By the time Norman Baker died, he was so reviled in his hometown that when his body arrived for burial in the family plot, the funeral director had to go to the local community college and pay six students $5.00 apiece to serve as pallbearers. And if the plaque mentioning Baker and his infamous radio station at the Mark Twain Overlook is really just a result of a little old-fashioned palm greasing, too, no one's talking.

The plaque is located at the Mark Twain Overlook on the hill just south of downtown Muscatine at Second and Brook Streets. For information call (563) 263–0241.

I O W A ' S   3 8 0 - M I L L I O N - Y E A R - O L D   S E A F L O O R   E X P O S E D !
N o r t h   L i b e r t y

The Great Flood of 1993 was the most significant flood event ever to occur in the United States, with seventy-five towns under floodwater, more than 10,000 homes completely destroyed, and total damages approaching $15 billion. To give you an idea just how much it rained, precipitation totals in eastern Iowa approached 48 inches between April 1 and August 31 (the yearly average for precipitation in the region is well below that, at 30–36 inches), with single storms dumping as much as 8 inches. Iowans, who love talking weather above all else, actually grew tired of talking about rain and flood.

Want a small silver lining in all those clouds and torrents? Well, floodwater surging over the emergency spillway at Coralville Lake in North Liberty eroded a 15-foot-deep channel in underlying bedrock deposits, uncovering a large swath of Devonian Age seafloor chock-full of fossils. More than ten years and half a million dollars of wise investment later, there's now a visitor and learning center at the site to help you hunt for corals and crinoids on the oldest ocean floor you're likely ever to peer at intently on your hands and knees.

How old an ocean floor is it? About 380 million years, give or take a million. The exposed limestone bedrock contains excellent fossil remains of some of the earliest Iowans, the relatively unglamorous marine life that inhabited the shallow tropical sea covering the region. Look for brachiopods (which appear to be the great-great-great-great- (and so on) grandparents of clams), crinoids, or "sea lilies," slender, segmented stems that were once rooted to the seafloor, and various forms of coral. The Coralville Lake Spillway offers a rare chance to get to know some of the oldest locals in these parts, courtesy of one of the worst natural disasters in U.S. history.

Coralville Lake is 5 miles north of Iowa City on Dubuque Street. The Spillway is just before the dam. Open during daylight hours. Admission is free.

MECCA FOR TREKKIES
Riverside

Ever wonder why the USS *Enterprise,* the spaceship from the TV show *Star Trek,* undertook such a long and dangerous journey? Why all the expense and trouble and the five long years, why the countless teleporter and warp-drive headaches for Scotty down in engineering, why all of Captain Kirk's torn polyester shirts, and, most important, why all the fraternizing with hordes of heavily makeupped, scantily clad alien women? Was it really just "to explore strange new worlds, to seek out new life forms and new civilizations, to boldly go where no man has gone before"?

Of course not. It was to help Captain Kirk get the heck out of Iowa. According to Gene Rodenberry's book, *The Making of Star Trek,* Captain James T. Kirk "was born in a small town in the state of Iowa" in the year 2228, and by the year 2250 Kirk was a Starfleet graduate on his first assignment, out of town, out of state, out of the galaxy, and getting farther away from home every minute.

Riverside, just east of Kalona, is the small Iowa town that claims the official, lucrative but dubious privilege of being the future birthplace of the smirking, leg-crossing fictional hero all too anxious to put as many light years as possible between himself and his old eastern Iowa stomping grounds. After contacting Rodenberry about the idea in 1985 at the prompting of a local *Trek* fan, the town council received a certificate from the show's creator confirming Riverside's birthplace status by dint of the fact that they were the first town to ask. Now, every summer on the last Saturday in June, Riverside celebrates Trek Fest, and thousands of *Star Trek* fanatics, or Trekkies, travel to town to dress up as Klingons and Starfleet officers, watch

Though it might look like a famous starship, licensing
fees can be outrageous. It's really the USS Riverside.

videos of the show, hold fan-club meetings, buy and sell show
memorabilia, drink beer, and have a parade down Main Street.

The town hoped to construct a bronze bust of Kirk to give
due homage to their future wanderer, but Paramount wanted a
$40,000 licensing fee to use Kirk's future likeness, and that
was that. Instead, they built their very own starship, the USS
Riverside (a station-wagon-size *Enterprise* knockoff), and set it
down on a trailer in a small park downtown, as if the teleporter weren't working and the crew had been forced to make a
rare trailer landing.

Young people have been leaving small towns in Iowa in search of who knows what greener pastures for decades; many leave for Minneapolis or Chicago, some go much farther, and some even return home eventually to enjoy the very same things that, as teenagers, they couldn't wait to leave. But Riverside asked for the honor of helping to inspire a future son to travel farther from Iowa than any man has ever been. The best we can hope for is that he at least remembers to call his poor mom back in Riverside to wish her happy birthday.

Riverside is located 13 miles south of Iowa City on Highway 22. You can't miss the 22-foot-long USS *Riverside* in the small park downtown. Trek Fest is held each year on the last Saturday in June. For more information call (319) 648–5475 or visit www.trekfest.com.

THE FINEST ROUND BARN AROUND
West Branch

Ever wonder what mid-nineteenth-century farmers argued about? Barns, for starters. More specifically, they debated the costs and benefits of round barns versus the tried and true rectangular variety. As part of a larger effort to promote more efficient and economical farming practices, Iowa State University encouraged area farmers and contractors to build round barns, but Iowans weren't so easily convinced. Was it mere folly to build in the round, or did a true round, or eight-, or sixteen-sided barn stand up to tornadoes better, as well as offer more storage space bang for the materials buck? (And that debate, my friends, might be indicative of the excitement of life on a nineteenth-century Iowa farm.)

Just take a glance at almost any barn still around, and you'll know which side (or how many sides) won. In Iowa the squares have it by a long shot. Between 1830 and 1920 farmers built an estimated 100,000 barns in the state, but only 180 were round or multisided. At present, barns are reported to be disappearing from the Iowa landscape at the rate of about 1,000 per year, and only about a hundred of the round and multi-sided barns remain.

The Secrest Octagonal Barn, located just west of Downey, is said to be one of Iowa's largest and finest remaining round barns. (Of course, it's not really round but eight-sided. In Iowa, though, more than four sides earn a barn honorary round status.) Built in 1883 by a master builder with the unlikely name of George Longerbeam (we didn't make that up), the barn is 80 feet tall and once held more than two hundred tons of hay in the loft, along with thirty-two horses, sixteen cows, and farm implements galore in the lower level. It also features classic red vertical siding, a sectional bell-shaped roof, and an octagonal cupola that sits six stories above the barnyard.

Thanks to the efforts of a local professor, Richard Tyler, and scores of volunteers, the barn is in sound round shape for its age. Just pull up and take a gander. There are no regular tours because it's not a business but a private passion shared by Tyler and a select group of interested citizens. If you show up, you've automatically joined the latter group. Don't be shy; the owner is used to having company. But be forewarned. If you stay around much longer than half an hour, he'll probably slap a bucket in your hand and put you to work.

The Secrest Barn is located at 5750 Osage Street, about 10 miles east of Iowa City and 5 miles south of West Branch. From Iowa City head east on US 6 about 5 miles. At the bend in the road turn left on Oasis Road. Go 1 mile and turn right on Osage Street. Barn will be 1 mile on left.

HOOVER'S MORNING MEDICINE
West Branch

There are most certainly some benefits to being the president of the United States. When West Branch's most famous son, Herbert Hoover, began his term in 1928, he was a little chunky, about 210 pounds on a 5 foot 11 inch frame. But instead of scolding him, or telling him to cut carbs (did they know about carbs back then?), his physician, Joel T. Boone, invented a game to help Hoover stay trim and even invited his cabinet to play it with him, first thing every morning (except Sundays, of course).

And what a game it was. Christened "Hoover Ball" by a *New York Times* reporter, it consisted of teams of two to four, an 8-foot-high net, a 66-foot by 30-foot court, and a six-pound medicine ball. The rules were simple: Catch the ball on your side of the net (trying not to grunt) and throw it immediately back over at your opponents, preferably as hard and fast as humanly possible. The *Des Moines Register* caught the spirit of the game when it reported: "The effect is that of a group of travelers tossing their luggage at a boat that has just pulled away from the dock, only to have the crew heave it right back again." Scored just like tennis but decidedly less genteel, Hoover Ball became something of a sensation during Hoover's term—people were throwing medicine balls at one another all across the country.

Hoover and his so-called "Medicine Ball Cabinet" were fanatical about the game. Each morning, rain or shine, a group of four to eighteen dignitaries (with an average age of fifty-three) showed up on the White House lawn dressed in flannel shirts, leather jackets, and old trousers and played Hoover Ball until the 7:30 A.M. whistle blew at a factory nearby. "We paid no

attention to the weather except for a very heavy rain," wrote
Secretary of the Interior Ray Lyman Wilbur. "We played in cold
and wind, snow and rain, and in the four years we were driven
indoors only two or three times [to play in the White House
basement!] because of an unusually drenching downpour."
Reports had it that Hoover was a "lusty" Hoover Ball player,
with a mean forehand drive, but that Supreme Court Justice
and former Columbia football star Harlan F. Stone was a positive menace. "When he hurls them," one observer claimed,
"they stay hurled."

But enough of history. Hoover Ball is still alive and well,
right here in West Branch. Every August during Hooverfest, a
celebration in honor of President Hoover's birthday, they hold
the Hoover Ball National Championships. Anyone—that's right,
even you—can field a team and compete for a national title in
either the four-pound or six-pound medicine-ball categories. Or,
of course, if getting hit in the gut over and over again with a
medicine ball isn't your idea of a good time, you can just go
and cheer on your favorite lusty Hoover Baller.

And how good was Hoover Ball at keeping Hoover trim? He
dropped to a svelte 185 during his term and never missed a
day of work due to illness or medicine-ball-related injury. Still,
some people aren't sold on the game. *Sports Illustrated* complained that heaving a six-pound ball back and forth over and
8-foot-high net "cannot be accomplished graciously." Though
that may be true, we know people will do far less gracious
things to drop a few pounds. For example, have you ever had
to watch someone eating a hamburger without a bun?

The Hoover Presidential Library in West Branch hosts
Hooverfest the first week of each August in honor of Hoover's
birthday. The Hoover Ball National Championships are held in
West Branch's Beranek Park. For more information or for
entry forms, call (800) 828–0475 or visit www.hooverassoc
.org/hooverballchampionships.htm.

BURRITOS AND STOCK CARS
West Liberty

The tiny town of West Liberty, about 20 miles east of Iowa City, has four Mexican restaurants (all excellent) as well as a combination Mexican bakery and Spanish-language video store filled with foreign films and foreign pastries. (We can vouch for the pastries but not for the movies.) Meatpacking has drawn thousands of Mexican immigrants to the town over the last two decades, and though West Liberty looks much like any other small Iowa town—red brick storefronts, tree-lined sidewalks, a small grocery on Main Street—the strong Latino influence, evident in everything from restaurants to shop signs (many are in Spanish), sets the tone.

That's not to say that some homegrown "culture" doesn't remain to give the town a diverse mix of diversions. If you're ever downtown on an early summer evening, take your burrito (and movie for later) and wander over a few blocks to the fairgrounds. Don't worry, you won't need directions; just follow the deafening roar and the hazy glow from the stadium lights to the Muscatine County Fairgrounds Track, a half-mile dirt-track speedway that will get your heart beating faster than a three-jalapeño salsa.

At $9.00 admission is a little pricey, but it's worth it. Pick a place at the far end of the bleachers, as close to the concrete abutment as crowd control will allow. Then, as the race cars hurtle into the turn at speeds of more than 90 miles an hour, they'll be headed straight for you. And when they start their slides and inch up on two wheels (they really do) as they round the bend, the roar of the engines will fill your head, the earth beneath your feet will seem to rumble, and you'll have to try hard not to scream. Ay caramba!

From Iowa City head east on US 6 about 20 miles. Turn right at the light at the center of town. Follow the roar to the Muscatine County Fairgrounds.

WHAT'LL IT BE? A DIPSY DOODLE OR A HADACOL?
Wilton

First established in 1867 and billed as the nation's oldest continuously operating soda fountain, the Wilton Candy Kitchen offers visitors an almost surreal dose of authentic Americana, which is a fancy way of saying that the place is so real it's unreal. Little has changed in the shop since the 1920s, when the current owner, George Nopoulos, started working for his father at the age of six, winding the Brunswick record player to keep customers entertained. The high, stamped-tin ceiling, white marble countertops (burnished by more than one hundred years of elbow rubbing), walnut booths, leaded-glass light fixtures, chrome-plated fountain spigots, and old-time lunch counter make you feel as though you've stepped right into a Hollywood vision of what a small-town ice-cream parlor should be. But, wonder of wonders, instead of some designer reproduction, it's the rare genuine article.

Even rarer still, the ice-cream parlor is run by the same couple who were serving up vanilla phosphate and grilled cheese just after World War II. Thelma Nopoulos started washing dishes at the soda fountain when she was only ten years old, but she and George didn't marry until 1949. Their fathers, both Greek immigrants, couldn't help but play matchmakers, but it wasn't until after George returned from service overseas that "sparks began to fly behind the soda fountain." Thelma is now the charming hostess who'll step from behind the counter to chat about anything from local history (she published a book on Wilton history recently) to politics.

And, more than fifty years later, magic is still happening behind that very same soda fountain. What kind of magic, you dare ask? Just for starters, they've got Black Cows and Green Rivers on the menu. Never heard of them? Well, the Wilton Candy Kitchen is a veritable living museum of long-forgotten concoctions sure to make you swoon. How about a strawberry phosphate or a cherry Coke? Or, if you're feeling more daring, why not order a Pink Lady (strawberry, cherry, and vanilla flavorings), a Hadacol (root beer and cola), or a Dipsy Doodle (six different flavors mixed together).

Each and every concoction is made from water carbonated on the premises, syrup, and George's very own homemade ice cream. The place is so authentic, politicians have taken to stopping by on their forays through eastern Iowa in hopes that some of the Nopoulos charm will rub off on them. But don't let that deter you from visiting—the politicians never stick around for long. And, ever conscious of image, they never dare get caught on camera with a Pink Lady or Dipsy Doodle, so there'll be plenty left over for you and a sweetheart.

The Wilton Candy Kitchen is located at 310 Cedar Street in downtown Wilton, just south of US 6, midway between Iowa City and Davenport; (563) 732–2278. It's still open seven days a week, as it has been ever since 1910.

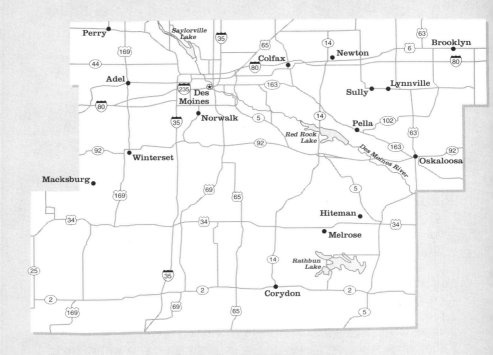

SOUTH CENTRAL

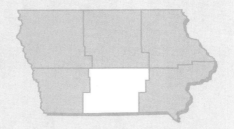

SOUTH CENTRAL

PLEASE PASS THE FIVE TONS OF SWEET CORN
Adel

"Corn's tricky," says Steve Amundsen of Moline, Illinois. "One person's fully eaten ear isn't the same as another person's fully eaten ear." Forgive him for waxing philosophical, but Amundsen was caught up in the excitement of watching a round of competition in the Corn Eating Contest at Adel's Sweet Corn Festival, held each summer on the second Saturday in August. And really, you couldn't help but agree he had a point. Even to an observer not inclined to philosophy, it was clear that some corn eaters were being a bit more conscientious about clearing the cob than others. (A few participants chomping their way through their allotment of ears seemed to be doing more corn spreading than a John Deere in springtime.) "It's not like a hot-dog-eating contest," Steve mused. "A hot dog is eaten, or it isn't. But corn on the cob is a whole nother story."

Rather than get caught up in the nearly impossible technicalities of fairly judging a corn eating contest, though, we decided to join the estimated 10,000 other festival gorgers, I mean, goers, for a few pieces of the more than five tons of Deardorf sweet corn served up—with healthy dollops of butter and loads of napkins—on Adel's beautiful town square. Dominated by a 1902 château-style county courthouse, Adel's square is where the whole festival unfolds: Vendors sell food and crafts on the sidewalks, bands and dance groups perform on

the Court House Square Stage, townspeople and out-of-towners
mix in the beer garden and dance in the square streets until
midnight, and, of course, eaters with a competitive streak buzz
through more than their fair share of Iowa's favorite crop.

Just a word of caution, though: It might be wise to steer
clear of the Raccoon Valley Bank parking lot the Friday night
before the Sweet Corn Festival. That's where the shucking
takes place, and, no surprise here, with 10,000 pounds of corn
to husk, they're always looking for enthusiastic volunteers. In
lieu of those, however, any warm body will do.

Adel is located on U.S. Highway 169 north of I–80. The
Sweet Corn Festival takes place the second Saturday in August,
right on the courthouse square. For more information call
(515) 993–5472.

Is This the United Nations? Nope, It's Iowa
Brooklyn

Not every small town in rural America raises the flag of
the United Nations—a baby blue globe perched atop lau-
rels against a field of white—on Main Street, but tiny Brooklyn
did, and the residents didn't even come close to stopping there.
Ireland's green, white, and gold hangs in front of the offices of
the town rag, the *Brooklyn Chronicle,* the Union Jack stirs in
the breeze just outside the door of Osborne Real Estate and
Insurance, and a green-and-red flag with a shield in the center
that we've yet to positively identify graces the pole in front of
the local watering hole, the Front Street Tap. You don't have to
look hard to find Italy, France, Germany, and Australia, too,
among some of the more esoteric flags, all lined up as if

Anyone up for playing Guess That Flag?
Photo: Catherine Cole

waiting for an Olympic parade to roll down the streets of Brooklyn's sleepy red-brick downtown.

The brain-seed of Alex Whorley, a transplanted New York businessman looking for a way to wave customers off I–80 into Brooklyn's struggling downtown, the flags are paid for not by tax dollars but through sales. In the dead center of town is a shop selling flags and memorabilia, as well as local knick-knacks on consignment. Staffed by volunteers, the store's proceeds support the maintenance and replacement of all the flags, including a monstrous 20-foot by 38-foot Old Glory, flanked by flags from all fifty states, which flies day and night, rain and shine, atop an 80-foot pole behind the volunteer fire department. If you're lucky, Helga Rhinehart, the mayor's wife, will be working the store's counter, and she might tell you about Mr. Whorley's attempt a few years back to sell the old bridge, that is, "The Brooklyn Bridge" to the interstate, on eBay. She won't even crack a smile when she tells you that a woman offered the town $50,000 for its Brooklyn Bridge, but no one could figure out a way to move it, so they simply tore it down after they built the new one. (If you believe that, I bet they've still got a little bridge they'd be willing to sell you in Brooklyn, Iowa.)

If you listen to Mrs. Rhinehart's voice as she spins her stories, you might pick up just a hint of an accent, so slight it makes you want to pay closer attention, to really hear its beautiful lilt. And if you're nosy enough to ask, she'll tell you she moved to Brooklyn from Germany more than forty years ago. "Still read German newspapers, though," she says, with a hint of pride in her voice. Then, when she invites you to sign the shop's guest book, you might consider how fittingly American Brooklyn's downtown really is.

Brooklyn is located just off I–80, midway between Des Moines and Iowa City, at mile marker 197.

THE HOTEL HARD WATER BUILT
Colfax

The historic former Hotel Colfax, nestled in the hills on the eastern edge of town, is now home to Teen Challenge of the Midlands, a Christian-based drug-and-alcohol-treatment facility for teens. But in the late nineteenth century, this old three-story hotel once played host to the well-to-do infirm who came to Colfax in search of the area's famed mineral water, reputed to have almost miraculous medicinal properties.

A firm prospecting for coal in the area discovered Colfax's mineral waters in the fall of 1875, and after thirsty workmen noticed the water tasted much different from the water in other town wells, it was sent to Chicago for chemical analysis. Tests showed the water contained high concentrations of calcium, magnesium, potassium, bicarbonate, and sodium; in other words, the water was in need of a little softening. Of course, in the nineteenth century, people were less concerned with stained toilet bowls, clogged pipes, and poor soap lather in the shower (there wasn't a whole lot of indoor plumbing back then) than they were with treating a myriad of still mysterious ailments for which there were no proven remedies.

Not long after the Colfax mineral waters were discovered, people who drank (and people who bottled) the water claimed it a cure-all for everything from arthritis to angina. By 1876 a small hotel was built to accommodate mineral-water-seeking visitors, in 1878 the three-story Hotel Colfax was dedicated, and in 1884 a 300-room hotel (expanded to 500 rooms in 1909) was built on the bluff overlooking town. There were so many visitors coming to drink the waters and soak in the hot mineral-water baths that the town built a rail line from the train depot, 1 mile east of Colfax, up the hill to the hotel. By 1892 the water's fame had grown so much that President Grover Cleveland's personal physician recommended he drink Colfax mineral water for his stomach problems and had barrels of it shipped to the White House.

Whereas the mineral waters used to be the big draw in town, now Colfax's Trainland U.S.A. tempts travelers off the interstate by the thousands each summer. A labor of love by Leland "Red" Atwood, Trainland consists of more than twenty simultaneously operating toy trains, 25,000 feet of wire, 200 miniature buildings, 2,600 square feet of display area, and a mile's worth of track. The exhibit contains various classic scenes of Americana in miniature, all painstakingly hand-painted by Red himself, including Mount Rushmore, the Statue of Liberty, trolley cars in San Francisco, and an operating drive-in movie. And at Trainland you'll meet a man with a passion for trains as huge as his train set—Red tore down his old home so that he could build a new one better able to accommodate his trains.

The old Hotel Colfax, now Teen Challenge of the Midlands, is located on the eastern edge of town at 900 North League Road. Trainland U.S.A. is located at 3135 Highway 117, North Colfax, and is open Memorial Day to Labor Day from 9:00 A.M. to 7:00 P.M. and by appointment other times of the year. For more information or to make an appointment, call (515) 674–3813.

A TOAST TO THE TIME WE GOT ROBBED
Corydon

If you want some proof that time heals all wounds, then allow us to offer exhibit A: Corydon's Jesse James Days, held each year on the first Friday and Saturday in June. The celebration, which includes the three big Bs of Iowa festivaldom—beer garden, bands, and barbecued meats—is held to commemorate the robbing of Corydon's Ocobock Bank of somewhere between $6,000 and $10,000, depending on whom you ask. And, in case you hadn't guessed, the festival is called Jesse James Days because Jesse James, along with his brother Frank, Cole Younger, and Clell Miller, did the robbing.

A few days before an important town meeting, Jesse and his gang arrived in town posing as cattle buyers, apparently the modern-day equivalent of traveling salesmen. The day of the meeting, on June 3, 1871, most of the townspeople were gathered at the Methodist church, so the four outlaws attracted little notice as they rode into town on horseback dressed in linen dusters. Their first stop was the County Treasurer's Office, its safe piled high with recent tax collections, at the northeast corner of Corydon's town square. Town legend has it that Jesse James asked the junior clerk if he could make change for a $100 bill as a ploy to get him to open the safe, but the clerk said that the safe was locked and that the county treasurer, who held the keys, had gone to town meeting. To help Jesse James get his change, he directed him 1 block west to the Ocobock Bank. (Talk about telling the lion where the lambs sleep.)

The gang found the Ocobock Bank tended by a single lonely clerk and forced him to open the safe with either the old "Got change for $100 bill?" trick, or the old "You've got a gun in your face. Open the vault now." trick, historians aren't sure which. At any rate Jesse and his gang made off with somewhere around $8,000 (give or take $2,000) of the townspeople's money. Legend even has it that the gang was so disappointed by how easy the heist was that they showed up at the town meeting to taunt the crowd with the fact that they had just robbed their bank. At first everyone thought it was a hoax, but when word came from the clerk that the bank had indeed been robbed, citizens formed a posse and pursued the James gang all the way into Missouri before losing the trail.

And now, 132 years and a lot of water under the bridge later, Corydon celebrates the day it was an easy target to a

famous outlaw. If you happen to miss the celebration, you can
still get your Jesse James fix at the Prairie Trails Museum,
where there is a display of the actual safe that James robbed
inside a re-creation of Ocobock Bank, as well as various other
James artifacts.

The lesson here? You know something's history when it no
longer stings. So raise a glass with Corydon citizens in honor of
getting the shakedown and then having it rubbed in your face.

In June, July, and August the Prairie Trails Museum,
located on Highway 2 in Corydon, is open weekdays and Saturdays from 10:00 A.M. to 5:00 P.M. and Sundays from 1:00 to
5:00 P.M. In April, May, September, and October, the museum is
open daily from 1:00 to 5:00 P.M. For more information call
(641) 872–2211. The Ocobock Bank was located on the square
where Citizens Bank now stands. The eastern exterior wall of
the bank is affixed with a plaque marking the historic site.

A BIKE RIDE THROUGH THE COUNTRY
WITH 20,000 FRIENDS
Des Moines

In 1973, the first year the *Des Moines Register* sponsored a
bicycle ride across the entire state of Iowa, 300 people
showed up for the start, and a total of 114 riders made the
entire distance. (Did the rest give up when they found the state
wasn't as flat as they imagined?) Thirty years later, the *Register's* Annual Great Bicycle Ride Across Iowa (RAGBRAI, pronounced rag-bry) is now the oldest, longest, largest, and
possibly best-fed (you didn't think Iowans would bike all day
without the promise of pork for dinner, did you?) bicycle-
touring event in the world, so popular that officials now limit
the number of weeklong participants to 8,500 to maintain a

semblance of sanity. With day-trippers joining in around urban centers like Des Moines, the pedaling, Lycra-clad ranks can swell to five figures: An estimated 23,000 bikers rode from Boone to Des Moines during RAGBRAI XVI, a group that, were they to incorporate themselves as a town (how about Saddle-soreville for a name?), would be about the twenty-seventh largest in the state.

The ride began as a kind of challenge between *Des Moines Register* writers (and avid cyclists) John Karras and Don Kaul. Karras suggested to Kaul that he ride his bike across Iowa and write columns about his experiences along the way. Kaul told Karras he would do it but on one condition; that Karras ride with him. Karras, of course, agreed. They got approval from the paper's managing editor, offered an invitation to *Register* readers to join them on the trip (only six weeks before they were scheduled to set out), and RAGBRAI was born.

One of the more eccentric participants that first year was Clarence Pickard, an eighty-three-year-old from Indianola. His touring bicycle of choice? A used ladies Schwinn. His workout gear to keep comfortable in the late-August heat? Long woolen underwear, long pants, a long-sleeved shirt, and a silver pith helmet. Pickard completed the entire ride, including the 110-mile leg from Des Moines to Williamsburg in 100-degree (F)-plus heat, and became a favorite with readers.

A mixture of town parade, big block party, and endurance test, RAGBRAI is essentially a different bike ride every summer. Each year ride planners lay out the west to east route to pass through different towns; by its thirtieth year, RAGBRAI had passed through all ninety-nine Iowa counties and about 80 percent of its incorporated towns. Though the variety is surely appreciated by return participants, there may have been another factor. As hospitable as Iowans are, a crowd of 8,500 hungry, thirsty bikers returning every July—filling the hotels, restaurants, bars, bathrooms, campgrounds, bedrooms, and lawns—might be too much for any town to handle.

For information and application go to www.ragbrai.org or call (800) 474–3342.

A COLLECTION OF CHOKERS
Des Moines

The biggest mystery surrounding Dr. James Downing's collection of objects removed from his patients' food and airway passages isn't necessarily why he would collect and label such specimens (chalk it up to good recordkeeping), but what exactly half the items are. Sure, many of them are common household objects, including coins of every denomination (with pennies and dimes particular favorites), buttons, safety pins, the odd chicken bone or shell fragment here and there. But a fairly large percentage of the collection is almost impossible to positively identify by sight alone.

The choke collection, contained in two large glass specimen cases (with objects removed from the bronchi nicely separated from objects removed from the esophagus), is the centerpiece of the Iowa Historical Museum's "Medical Marvels" exhibit. One of the state's first doctors to use a flexible instrument (bronchoscope) affording access to a patient's esophagus and bronchi, Dr. Browning practiced for many years in Des Moines and supposedly collected and displayed the objects to discourage patients from putting things in their mouths. But it's likely that Browning wasn't just interested in educating the public; he also had a wicked sense of humor. One of Browning's nickel-swallowing pediatric patients received these instructions on her discharge orders: "Feed her anything but nickels and pennies."

One final mystery of the collection is why there are so many safety pins. After a rough count I estimated there were somewhere between twenty-five and thirty safety pins of all shapes and sizes in the collection. Why were so many people swallowing safety pins back in the 1930s? Was it some bizarre parlor trick that's long since passed out of fashion? Turns out it was just one of the hazards of being a mom or dad before disposable diapers came along. A diaper-changing mom would put a safety pin or two in her mouth, make one wrong swallow, and then be on her way to Dr. Browning's to become, in a very small way, a part of medical history.

The museum is located downtown in the Iowa Historical Building, 600 East Locust Street. Take the East Sixth Street exit off I-235 to Locust. For more information call (515) 281-5111.

HEAD-ON JOE'S SHOW
Des Moines

Joseph "Head-on Joe" Connolly couldn't take credit for coming up with the idea of running two train engines straight into each other at high speeds for the edification and entertainment of large paying crowds. (But then again, coming up with an idea like that is a dubious distinction.) That honor falls to a Mr. William Crush, Vice President of the Missouri, Kansas, and Texas Railroad, who dreamed up a rather dramatic way of putting to rest his company's old locomotives while making some money at the same time. In 1896 the appropriately named Mr. Crush staged his first, and last, head-on locomotive collision for a group of paying customers in Missouri, among them one Joseph Connolly. The end result? A terrific crash (as expected), an extremely large double-boiler explosion (unexpected), and two spectators dead and many more wounded.

Joseph Connolly might have come away from the event an anti-train wreck activist. Instead, he brought head-on trainwreck madness to the Iowa State Fair. It took him some work to get the Fair Board to agree, but after he offered to assume all risk and liability, they signed off on the idea. The first Iowa State Fair train wreck was staged in 1897, the second in 1921, and the third and final one in 1932, which drew more than 35,000 spectators. This last wreck, reportedly the most dramatic, was a head-on collision between the *Roosevelt* and the *Hoover*. (Hoover was battling Roosevelt to hold onto his presidency at the time.) According to Floyd Deets, superintendent of the fairgrounds from the 1940s until 1985 and a firsthand observer of the 1932 crash, workers removed the seats from the coaches, loaded the front of the locomotives with dynamite, and set tanks of kerosene inside so that the trains would explode and burst into towering flames upon impact. "There was a challenge as to which engineer would jump out last," he said. "But since one was going downhill at a pretty good clip, and the other was working pretty hard to go uphill, the engineer going down must have had to jump earlier."

The trains crashed, both *Roosevelt* and *Hoover* went down in flames, and the mild-mannered Midwesterners loved it. Joseph Connolly might not have come up with the idea himself, but he sure knew good, clean catastrophic fair-time fun when he saw it.

The Iowa State Fairgrounds Museum displays a bell from the 1932 train, as well as photographs of the wreck. But alas, they no longer stage wrecks. Take I–80 to exit 141 (U.S. Highway 65), and then take US 65 south to exit 79. Follow University Avenue west to the fairgrounds. For more information about the fair, call (800) 545–3247 or visit www.iowastatefair .org.

A SANDWICH HOT ENOUGH TO SEND YOU
TO THE HOSPITAL
Des Moines

You could win from $500 to $10,000 for eating an entire barbecue sandwich at Big Daddy's Bar-B-Q in Des Moines. The hotter the sandwich's sauce, the more money you win.

Before you take a bite, however, both your doctor and your lawyer must sign a notarized form releasing Big Daddy (a.k.a. Ike Seymour) from any legal liability pertaining to the results of your attempt. And you need to let Big Daddy know your local hospital of choice so it can have paramedics on hand. This should give you a clue that these are not your average hot sauces.

They have names like Are You a Survivor?, Help! and Emergency Room (where most contestants end up). Just a drop on the end of a toothpick leaves even the most macho of diners sweaty, breathless, and hiccuping.

If you eat an entire sandwich with the Big Daddy's Bar-B-Q sauce of your choice on it in five minutes and keep it down for thirty minutes, you win. Only one person has ever done this. That was back in 1996, and he, too, was eventually rushed to the hospital.

"The doctors at Des Moines General say, 'Why did you do it? You know Big Daddy's got a hot sauce?'" Big Daddy reports. "The visit costs them more than the challenge."

Challenge entry fees range from $200 to $4,000, payable in the form of a cashier's check to the elementary school or grocery store of your choice. (Big Daddy is an avid crusader against hunger and a prolific donor to the Food Bank of Iowa.)

Unfortunately, Big Daddy's restaurant was closed at press time, allowing Big Daddy to concentrate on catering and retail sales of his sauces. He hopes the closing is temporary. If you want to accept the hot-barbecue-sandwich-eating challenge, call Big Daddy to get the necessary paperwork rolling. And if you stop by the restaurant when he's prepping for one of his many catering gigs, he'll be happy to feed you or give you a taste of one of his hottest barbecue sauces on the tip of a toothpick—no notarized form required.

Big Daddy's Bar-B-Q restaurant is located at 1000 East Fourteenth Street in Des Moines. His sauces are available in select Midwestern grocery stores and online at www.big daddysbbq.net. For more information call (515) 262–0352.

A SKYWALK WITH 18 HOLES
Des Moines

Des Moines isn't the only Midwestern city with skywalks to protect citizens from the fickle weather. But it may be the only city to host a three-course, 18-hole miniature golf tournament 20 feet above its streets.

Des Moines has more than 3 miles of skywalks downtown, where the nonprofit Downtown Community Alliance hosts the Skywalk Open on the first weekend in February. More than 1,800 people put their putting skills to the test on the skywalk carpets each year, making it the largest indoor golf tournament in the world. Local businesses and community groups sponsor individual holes, and participants compete in one of three divisions—singles, doubles, or foursomes—with prizes going to the top three finishers in each division.

In its seventeen years of existence, the tournament has gotten a lot of good press: *Midwest Living* called it "one of the best wintertime celebrations," and Festivals.com included it in its list of Greatest Events on Earth.

Though we're sure course officials have things under control, may we suggest some rules for the tournament? Recarpet all divots, no mulligans for balls lost under the heat registers, and no banging one's head against the skywalk glass upon missing a putt for birdie. It leaves smudge marks.

The Skywalk Open is held each year the first weekend in February. For more information call (515) 243–6625 or visit www.desmoinesdt.com.

P u n y   P a r k
H i t e m a n

*H*iteman is one of those towns carrying the warning that if you blink, you'll miss it. The list of what it doesn't have includes the small-town standards—a gas station, a bar, and a church. Hiteman doesn't even have a downtown to speak of, but it does have 101 residents and a claim to fame: Iowa's smallest park.

Keep your eyes wide open as you head into "town," turn south on Fourth Street and there it is, up ahead, where the gravel road splits into a Y, a roughly 10-by-20-foot plot of grass. Technically, it's just big enough to hold the entire town, and though it never has, it once held a wedding. A very small wedding.

The hand pump in the center of the park is the reason it exists. The pump dates back to the time when Hiteman was an active mining town and there were wells, spaced a block or so apart, that made up the public water supply. The use of wells stopped in the 1950s, though the one in what is now the park remained. When past residents came to visit, they took photos of the remaining pump for nostalgia's sake, so someone thought it would be nice to pretty it up with a paint job. Then

A park with picnic space for two.

Photo: Clint Buckner

Howard Thomas, who lives a few steps away from the park with his wife, Lois, stuck a bench near the pump. A park was born.

Over the years a flagpole flying the state and national flag was added. During the town's centennial in 1990, the Thomases' daughter made a sign, now mounted to the flagpole, reading, CITY PARK, HITEMAN, IOWA. The couple has taken over park landscaping as well. Lois added some plastic flowers in a pail (she says that real ones don't grow so well here), and Howard walks around the park every once in a while with a weed wacker, as the park is not big enough to hold a mower.

Once people noticed the park was shrinking, due to graters and tractors traveling the gravel roads surrounding it, Howard and some other neighborhood men got some bridge planks from the county and edged the park in. This act of conservation ensures Hiteman's claim to fame remains an attraction— for those who don't blink and then miss it.

Traveling south from Des Moines on Highway 5, turn west on 170th Street into Hiteman. Go south on Fourth Street, and you'll see the park straight ahead.

INVASION OF THE DOLLS
Lynnville

Norma Conover took up doll making as therapy when she was diagnosed with cancer back in 1979. She and husband Bruce made their first doll in 1980, poured their first ceramic molds, and started teaching doll-making classes in 1985. Now, twenty-three years and more than 600 dolls later, the Conovers haven't got much room left for themselves, let alone their visiting kids and grandkids, in their rambling 1870 farmhouse. And while the doll making may have helped Norma win her battle with cancer, now she's got a different, though much less pressing challenge—how to stop making them. "You know what hobbies tend to do," Norma said. "They take over. Sometimes now we call it a disease."

"We have dolls throughout the whole house," Norma told me at the beginning of the tour, which proved a bit of an understatement. Imagine an extremely overstocked doll shop with a Victorian flair; now imagine that the owner had to sell and move her whole inventory into her living room, dining room, hallways, and bedrooms, and that should give you a good idea of what the Conover place looks like. It's as if the house has been invaded by an army of cheerful, orderly, extremely well-dressed Victorian munchkins. And Norma and Bruce made every single one of them.

The dolls come in various shapes and sizes, with outfits ranging from a black-velvet winter coat and fur muffler to a frilly pink party dress. There are lots of pastel colors, of course, and pink predominates, probably because the majority of the dolls are girls. The most fascinating specimens are the "settings," or doll portraits, that Norma's done of close family members. Working from a baby picture, she finds a doll mold that closely approximates the appearance of the child, makes the doll, and then dresses it up to look exactly like the baby in the picture. Then she displays the doll right beside the picture, and voilà, she has a baby portrait filled with stuffing of someone dear to her heart. She's done one of her husband, her mother, and her aunt, her granddaughters, her two sisters, and even one of herself.

The Conovers have deep roots in Lynnville. Bruce's great-grandparents homesteaded the land back in 1853 and lived in a log cabin for seventeen years before building the farmhouse where the Conovers now house their dolls. And one of the fringe benefits of the Dollyville tour is that you get a thumbnail history of an original Iowa settler family and farmhouse along the way. If great-grandpa could only see his bedroom now.

That's a lot of unblinking eyes in one room.

From downtown Lynnville take First Street (right beside the gas station) west out of town. Head toward Scully for about 2 miles, then take the first right on a gravel road, East 132nd Street South. Follow the road about a quarter mile. (You'll have to make a quick right and then a quick left to stay on East 132nd Street South.) Dollyville will be the big white farmhouse on the left, 8099 East 132nd Street South. Visits are by appointment only. Call (641) 594–3449.

FLYING SKILLETS
Macksburg

The Macksburg National Skillet Throwing Contest started in the mid-1970s, and even though Kevin Jackson is one of fifteen Macksburg residents who plan the thing, he has no idea how it began. One can only imagine why throwing an iron skillet at a scarecrow for sport started, or why it took off as it did, but Kevin says that today's competition draws up to sixty teams of five. That's more than double the town's population of 140.

The idea is to throw the skillet at a set of three scarecrows, each with a piece of plastic-tile pipe for a neck. A basketball rests on the pipe. Contestants are awarded points for knocking the basketball off the pipe—5 points for a clean hit, square at the ball, and 1 point for anything the removes the basketball without hitting it directly. Underhand is the preferred throwing style, though some contestants mix it up with sidearm or overhand lobs. There's a three-sided cage around the scarecrows ever since two unfortunate competitors were hit with flying skillets a few years back—clean hits, by the way.

Sponsored teams come from Macksburg and neighboring towns. Kevin says there are even some annually returning teams from "down south" (Iowa, that is) as well as Colorado and beyond. Once a group from Japan happened upon the contest and entered. "They was real nice people, but they wasn't real big and just not strong enough," Kevin reports.

A festival is built around the contest, which includes a parade, a flea market, food vendors, and, for the kids, a pedal-tractor pull and a greased-pig contest. Another draw: Chicken Bingo, where you pay a dollar to put your name on one of sixty-four spots on a piece of plywood. A chicken is let loose on the plywood, and if it poops on your name, you win half the pot. A sweet victory, yes, but not nearly as sweet as winning the celebration's most sought-after title: Skillet Throwing Champion of America.

The Macksburg Festival's National Skillet Throwing Contest takes place each June on the Saturday before Father's Day. To get to Macksburg take I–80 west of Des Moines to Highway 169 south. Turn West on G61 just south of Winterset. For more information call Kevin at (641) 768–2291.

A LITTLE TOWN WITH A LOT OF IRISH
Melrose

Want to kiss the Blarney Stone but only have time and cash for a day trip to, say, southern Iowa? Well, you've got the luck of the Irish on your side. There just so happens to be a piece of the Blarney Stone—the rock high in the battlements of Blarney castle that supposedly gives all who kiss it the "gift of the gab"—in the little town of Melrose, founded by Irish immigrants in 1882. Of course, the authenticity of the stone has never been verified by outside sources, and Melrose citizens most certainly inherited the Irish penchant for stretching the truth. Townspeople even claim that MELROSE'S OWN BLARNEY STONE, as it's inscribed, was brought to Iowa from Ireland by leprechauns during the potato famine. Likely story. Who were these leprechauns? What proof of their existence can Melrose offer? Death certificates, tax records, vintage emerald-green clothes in extremely small sizes? The story sounds good, but we want some hard evidence before planting our lips against any strange stones.

Melrose has always been Irish, but recent downtown renovations make the place look as Irish as its founders surely did. When their downtown of seven or eight buildings threatened to topple over, the whole town banded together, scared away the raccoons, hauled away tons of debris, rewired, reroofed, and then painted the exteriors using color schemes common on the Emerald Isle. As a finishing touch, volunteers made flower boxes adorned with shamrocks and hung them on the front of every building. They even placed leprechaun statues at strategic locations. The end result is a charming Main Street that highlights the town's heritage.

If you want more proof that the blood runs green in the veins of Melrose citizens, you need look no farther than the street signs. Every street name has something to do with Ireland: They've got Shamrock Street, Leprechaun Lane, Cork Street, Tralee Street, and Kells Avenue, to name just a few. And Melrose has the only town park in the state with a Gaelic name, Tolendol Park. (*Tolendol* means "meeting place.") With so much Irish around, it almost feels like sacrilege to doubt the authenticity of Melrose's Blarney Stone.

Melrose is located on Highway 68, just south of U.S. Highway 34. For information call (641) 932–5108.

EVEN HONEST ABE WRESTLED
Newton

According to Kyle Klingman, associate director of Newton's International Wrestling Institute and Museum, Frank Gotch is the reason for the beginning of Iowa's love affair with wrestling. Born in Humbolt in 1878, Gotch was discovered by a wrestler named Farmer Burns, a man famous for demonstrating his strength by dangling from a hangman's noose and dragging around a thirty-pound anvil tied to his neck (but never at the same time). At the turn of the century, professional wrestling was a legitimate sport that drew large crowds,

A museum for the grappler in you.

and George "the Russian Lion" Hackenschmidt was the undisputed champion of the world.

And then Frank Gotch came along. On April 3, 1908, Gotch defeated Hackenschmidt in a match that lasted two hours and three minutes. Iowans were swept up in Gotch-mania. Thousands of young boys read dramatic stories about their home-state hero and dreamt of being just like Frank. Iowa had become a wrestling state.

When a rematch was held on September 4, 1911, at Chicago's Comiskey Park in front of a crowd of 33,000, and Gotch once again defeated the Russian Lion, his status as a legendary Iowan was affirmed. In a bizarre side note to the story,

George Hackenschmidt quit wrestling after his defeat and hit the books. In 1949, at the age of seventy-one, he became so convinced of his brilliance that on a visit to New York City he challenged Albert Einstein to debate the world's problems. (Einstein didn't debate the former world champ, but he did deliver a counter-challenge: an hour or two of good old-fashioned grappling in leotards, just him and Hackenschmidt, *mano a mano*.)

You can find a full Gotch exhibit at the International Wrestling Institute and Museum, along with displays of more contemporary Iowa wrestling legends (including Gable, Sanders, and Brands), exhibits on wrestling in antiquity, hundreds of plaques featuring the names of every NCAA wrestling champ in every weight class for the last forty or fifty years, and all sorts of other grappling memorabilia. For fans of Dan Gable—a four-time NCAA championship wrestler at the University of Iowa, a 1972 Olympic champion who didn't lose a single Olympic point (the wrestling equivalent of winning Wimbledon without dropping a single game), a University of Iowa coach who won fifteen titles and earned a 131-2 Big Ten record— you'll find everything from childhood photographs and old newspaper articles to the scale at West Waterloo High on which wrestlers, including Gable, used to weigh in. For someone from out of state, it would be almost impossible to understand Iowa's passion for wrestling, and for Gable, without a visit to the International Wrestling Institute.

One favorite highlight of mine was a painting of Abe Lincoln wrestling a man named Jack Armstrong on a summer day in 1831. The match was reportedly a close one, and though no one knows for sure who came away the victor, Honest Abe looks very threatening, and very much on top of his game, in the painting. For some reason, though, he's not wearing ear protectors or a singlet. Get that boy some real equipment, and he could have been a contender. He could have been somebody. Maybe, if he was born fifty years later, he could have even wrestled for the Hawks.

The International Wrestling Institute and Museum, 1690 West Nineteenth Street South, is located about 100 yards north of I–80 in Newton. Head north from I–80 on Highway 14 and take a left at the first light. The institute is down the hill on the left. For information call (641) 791–1517.

N O R W A L K ' S   S U P E R S T A R   T W I R L I N G   C O A C H
N o r w a l k

I f you want to talk elite baton twirlers in Iowa, then you're talking about a serious legacy, Jan Stivers's legacy, that is. The fifty-four-year-old Norwalk native and owner of Norwalk Superstars Baton, Dance, and Gymnastics Center has coached the last four Iowa State baton twirlers, the last four University of Northern Iowa twirlers, and the last two University of Iowa twirlers, or Golden Girls as they're called, who receive full scholarships for their awe-inspiring abilities with the baton. (The University of Iowa and the University of Hawaii are the only two universities in the country offering full financial aid to their baton twirlers.) And more of Jan Stivers's incredibly talented twirlers are sure to come.

In case you haven't been to an Iowa State, University of Northern Iowa, or University of Iowa football game (you're not from around these parts, are you?), baton at the collegiate level is not the run-of-the-mill twirling you remember from child-hood. A college twirler performs a set routine for each song the marching band plays during the half-time and postgame shows, moving her way around the football field in a dramatic solo performance that is part dance, part gymnastics, and part baton twirling. Perhaps the most impressive moments come with the astoundingly high baton tosses: Stivers-trained twirlers regularly throw the baton 30, 40, 50 feet in the air, perform an elegant acrobatic feat while it flashes silver through the fall sky, and then gracefully catch the baton just before it embeds itself in the turf. Some twirlers will toss two or three batons at the same time; Julie Canterbury, World Champion Twirler, former University of Iowa Golden Girl, and one-time Stivers student, could even twirl a baton around her neck. Golden Girl performances are so mesmerizing that they can make the happenings on the gridiron pale a little in comparison.

So what's the secret to Jan's coaching success? Her main ingredients, she says, are lots of positive reinforcement and lots of fun. "I try hard to make practice as fun as I can. I'll have them twirl and toss water balloons, or make up silly games," she says. Stivers not only teaches the girls different twirling techniques and moves, but she also models for her students from a very young age how to artfully choreograph their own performances. "I ask them, 'What is this music telling you to do here?' and they begin to learn that, say, a crescendo, is telling them to do something spectacular." As for the many moves she has dreamt up for her girls, she says, "You never know what's going to come out of my head. I never know what's going to come out of my head. I've come up with some crazy ideas." Like twirling piano keys or animal bones, for starters.

And she never seems to tire of finding fresh ideas. Not long ago she went out for dinner with a group of twirling judges, and the women started demonstrating tricks with dinner knives. "We were a bunch of women twirling knives for each other, saying, 'Hey, have you seen this trick? What about this one?' Luckily, we were in a room that didn't have many people in it, so we didn't scare anybody off." The most important ingredients in Jan's success might just be an almost palpable passion for twirling and an even more palpable love for her girls. "I've been twirling for over fifty years. I still love it, I love the girls, and I'm still learning new things," Jan says. And she's still singlehandedly supplying the state of Iowa with its yearly requirement of phenomenally talented collegiate twirlers.

Norwalk is located on Highway 28 about 12 miles south of Des Moines east of I–34 (exit 65). Norwalk Superstars Baton, Dance, and Gymnastics Center is located just south of town off Highway 28 at 360 Wright Road. For information about classes call (515) 981–4298.

THE ECCENTRIC MILLIONAIRE OF MAHASKA COUNTY
Oskaloosa

George Daily lived in the dilapidated house across the street from Oskaloosa High School, shuffled around town in dirty, rumpled clothes, talked to almost no one, and spent his days reading the *Wall Street Journal* in the town's library, playing checkers on a park bench in central square, and scouring trash bins for rags, cardboard, and old tires to bring home. (In other words he was a little eccentric, even for an Iowan.) He was, some people claim, Oskaloosa's own Boo Radley, the recluse in Harper Lee's novel *To Kill a Mockingbird*. Some students were afraid of him and claimed that the old man would grab kids and they'd never be seen again.

Now, thanks in part to Daily's generosity, high-school students attend classes in a new building that adjoins a state-of-the art, 695-seat performing-arts center, George Daily Auditorium. (A bronze statue of Daily playing checkers sits out front of the auditorium.) The students have new cheerleading uniforms, new word processors in their English classes, new dugouts at the baseball field. One young man even got $25 to put toward guitar lessons.

When Daily died in 1993 at the age of eighty-four, he left a considerable sum of money—money few people in town

George gave Oskaloosa a big gift that keeps on giving.

dreamed he ever had—in trust for the benefit of Oskaloosa. How much money? More than $6 million, all from oil revenues generated on a small parcel of land his itinerant laborer father had bought in Ascension Parish, Louisiana, back in the 1920s. Now, ten years after his death, his trust has helped pay for 275 community projects all over town, from a new park—the old Daily home was torn down and turned into a community wild-flower garden—to a summer-theater camp for kids. Daily's trust is still worth more than $5 million, and trustees accept applications for grants year-round. But local groups applying for aid must pay for a portion of their projects themselves, because the fund is designed not to bankroll ideas outright but to jumpstart cooperative community initiatives.

With all the benefits Oskaloosa citizens receive from Daily's largesse, they've begun to feel an obligation to preserve the memory of their eccentric benefactor. Marilee DeCook started teaching her fifth graders about George Daily's life after receiving new computers for her classroom with help from the trust in 1995. In 1997 Oskaloosa unveiled the statue of George—dressed in jacket and baseball cap and sitting alone on a park bench looking down at a checkerboard—in front of his auditorium, and, most triumphantly, Iola Cadwallader interviewed many of the Oskaloosans who knew and cared for Daily, and she wrote a musical. *George!* premiered at the George Daily Auditorium, just beside the George Daily statue, in July 2002. As of yet there's no talk of changing Oskaloosa's name to Dailyville, but who knows? Six-million-dollar gifts can make people feel pretty darn grateful.

The George Daily Auditorium is located next to the Junior/ Senior High School at 1800 North Third Street. From downtown take US 63 north to O Avenue. Take a right onto O Avenue and then a left onto North Third Street. The Daily Auditorium will be on the right. For more information call (641) 672–0799.

M A Y   S H E   B E   S T U B B O R N   I N   P E A C E
O s k a l o o s a

Y ou've probably heard of a pet cemetery, a final resting place for Fifi and Fido, but what about a mule cemetery? (Sounds a little exclusive doesn't it? Why not let cows, hogs, and horses in, too?) Nelson Pioneer Farm, located just a few miles north of Oskaloosa on U.S. Highway 63, has what appears to be the state's only all-mule cemetery. You can't buy your favorite beast of burden a burial plot here, though, for at

Our dearly departed
beasts of burden.

least two reasons: (1)
The cemetery is a his-
toric site, and (2) since
two mules are already
interred on the rather
cramped 15-by-15-foot
grounds (bordered by a
small white picket
fence), there's no room
left for any other dearly
departed hybrids.

Nelson Pioneer Farm
is a collection of fifteen
historic buildings, including a schoolhouse, a log
cabin, a post office, and a
Quaker meetinghouse,
located on beautiful
grounds a few miles north
of Oskaloosa. The heart of the complex is the Nelson homestead, with its antebellum farmhouse and barn and, of course,
its mule cemetery. Each grave is marked by a simple rectangular wooden plaque painted white and rounded at the top cor-
ners to look like a gravestone. HERE LIES "JENNIE" one reads.
FAMOUS WHITE MULE THAT SERVED IN THE CIVIL WAR. BRANDED US.
DIED MARCH 1891 AGE 42 YEARS. OWNED BY DANIEL NELSON.

Becky, the only other mule buried in the cemetery (her
name is in quotation marks on her grave marker, too—maybe
the names were aliases?), was a white-haired Union artillery
mule that lived to be thirty-four. A Civil War veteran himself,
Daniel Nelson obviously felt indebted enough to his trusty
white mules to mark out for them a prime final resting place.
But what about Nelson's countless other animals? Where are

they buried? If you're looking for an explanation for the obvious favoritism, then you need look no further than the fact that all three served in the military during the same war. Maybe they performed acts of selfless bravery for one another in the heat of battle, perhaps they all shared a tent and told stories about their sweethearts back home, or perhaps they just shared water from a canteen now and then. Whatever their relationship was, one thing is sure. War brings men and their mules together in ways that cannot be explained.

The Nelson Pioneer Farm is open from mid-May to mid-October. Hours of operation are Tuesday through Saturday from 10:00 A.M. to 4:30 P.M. and Sunday from 1:00 to 4:30 P.M. Take US 63 north out of Oskaloosa to County Road T65 and follow the signs to the Pioneer Farm at 2294 Oxford Avenue. For more information call (515) 672–2989.

A *B* I G   D U T C H   *W* I N D M I L L   I N   *I* O W A
P e l l a

E ven if you're from Scranton or Hong Kong, you may already know Pella for its eponymous corporation, Pella Windows, the company headquartered in town that manufacturers high-quality windows. If you've never been to Pella, though, you're in for an ethnic surprise. A Dutch immigrant community founded by a small band of Hollanders in 1847, Pella has held tightly to its old-world heritage, especially downtown, with its colorful, European-style storefronts, authentic Dutch bakery, and towering Dutch windmill just east of the town square. The end result is like seeing a Midwestern gal dressed up in Dutch costume—a pretty sight, but you can't help but wonder if she wouldn't feel a little more comfortable in jeans and a T-shirt.

*Which tastes better,
Dutch- or Danish-
milled flour?*

The new Dutch windmill, officially known as the Vermeer Mill and Interpretive Center, is part of Pella's Historical Village, a collection of twenty-one historical buildings, including a log cabin, a blacksmith shop, a church, and the boyhood home of Pella's own little outlaw Wyatt Earp, who lived here until he was fifteen. Completed in July 2002, the 90-foot-tall windmill (with an impressive height of almost 124 feet when you measure all the way to the tip of the most upright blade) is the tallest working windmill in the United States. (Since the mill is in the heart of downtown Pella, it had to be built taller than surrounding buildings to catch the wind.) An international effort, the mill was built by a man from the Netherlands and then assembled on-site by two craftsmen from Holland. Village employees operate the mill, grinding wheat into flour that's used by local restaurants and bakeries. If you want to make your own, extremely authentic Dutch pastries, you can buy some of the mill's flour, tied up in an attractive souvenir bag, at the Historical Village's gift shop.

The Historical Village is home to not only the tallest working Dutch windmill in the United States, but also the smallest Dutch village. Be sure to check out the 1:24 scale Miniature Dutch Village, featuring eighty very small, steep-roofed Dutch buildings (some of which are elaborately furnished), a water-filled canal, a working train, and a whole lot of ¼₄-sized Hollanders dressed in very small but still quite authentic Dutch costumes.

Pella Historical Village is located just east of the town square at 507 Franklin Street. (Just walk toward the 90-foot-tall windmill.) January through March, the Village is open Monday through Friday from 9:00 A.M. to 5:00 P.M. and Saturday from 10:00 A.M. to 3:00 P.M.; April through December, it's open Monday through Saturday from 9:00 A.M. to 5:00 P.M. For more information call (641) 628–4311.

A BIKE RIDE THAT FEELS LIKE IT SOUNDS
Perry

Though RAGBRAI (the *Register's* Annual Bike Ride Across Iowa) may be a lot more famous, Perry's BRR (Bike Ride to Rippey) is a whole helluva lot colder. Held each year the first Saturday in February, the bike ride consists of a 26-mile trip over mostly flat terrain to neighboring Rippey and back. Sounds easy enough, no? But throw in a stiff head wind, sub-freezing temperatures, and drifting snow, and you've got yourself an adventure.

So what's the secret to survival? Some participants swear by the preventive medicine of a good stiff drink, preferably before, during, and after the ride to ensure the greatest benefits. Others simply revel in the pain of frozen noses and toes, like those Polar Bear Club members who wade (boldly or insanely, depending on the way you look at it) into the frigid Atlantic on New Year's Day. And still others swear by petroleum-based products. "It's really my feet that I worry about. Sometimes they go numb and it's like I'm pedaling two bricks," one participant wrote. The solution? Lots of Vaseline. "I smear Vaseline all over my feet, wrap them in plastic baggies, then put my socks on over that. It feels like I'm practicing safe sex with my shoes, but at least it keeps my toes from freezing."

Over the last quarter century, BRR (or BRRRRR as it's known some bitterly cold years) has become the essential warm-up for hundreds of RAGBRAI enthusiasts who just can't hold out 'til summer for a day of fun, food, drink(s), and, oh yeah, biking, on the back roads of Iowa. Could you please pass the Vaseline?

For more information about BRR, call the Perry Chamber of Commerce at (515) 465–4601.

WAGON WHEEL ART
Sully

At the age of eighty-seven, Leonard Maasdam, Iowa sorghum farmer, builder, and inventor, erected a 60-foot-tall sculpture made out of more than 200 steel wagon wheels on land he owned just north of Sully. The towering sculpture is an impressive accomplishment for anyone, let alone an octogenarian, but if the whole truth be known, Leonard had a little help from his friends. "He was putting together those old steel wheels," his

grandson Craig Maasdam told me, "and I'd come out at night
and start looking at his welds. And some weren't very good;
they were coming apart, and so I'd spend two, three, four
hours fixing 'em each night." And, apparently, Leonard Maasdam never knew.

According to his grandson the sculpture was "kind of a last
hurrah" for a man whose life was filled with tinkering, building, and inventing. Among his many accomplishments Maasdam built a sorghum mill (located a few miles down the road
from the wagon-wheel tree) out of parts salvaged from scrap
yards as far away as Chicago, invented a trenching machine
with Gary Vermeer (called the Vermeer Trencher) used for laying tile in farm fields to improve drainage, helped perfect
something called the Pella Irrigation System, and built two
underground round houses just north of Pella that can be
heated and cooled with mind-boggling efficiency.

Maasdam's first passion was sorghum farming, though,
and his recycled-parts sorghum mill—he even made use of the
back end of an old car—is now the largest operating sorghum
mill in the United States and possibly the world. In case you're
like me and don't quite know what sorghum is, it's a sweet
syrup made from the juice of the sorghum plant. Don't confuse
it with molasses, though. As Craig Maasdam told me,
"Molasses is just the junk that's left over after they refine
sugar from sugar cane." Leonard's daughter, son-in-law, and
grandson Craig now run the mill and produce more sorghum
than anyone in the world.

Maasdam got the idea for a sculpture made out of wagon
wheels during one of his many trips to Wisconsin delivering
sorghum. "It was different from the one he built, not nearly as
big and a whole different shape, but that's where he got the
idea." But, apparently, Leonard didn't get caught up in technicalities when talking about his creation. "He just said he came
up with the idea himself. But I know he saw one in Wisconsin
because he showed me the postcard of the thing." One of his
daughters, Marge Kramer, has written a book about him called
The Man Behind the Mill, and according to Craig, "Not every-

Taking wagon wheel art to new heights.

thing is true and correct in the book, but most of it, 95 percent of it, is true. Some stuff he [Leonard] just got confused on."

L. J. Maasdam died in April 2003 at the age of ninety-eight. "He didn't do much after that wagon-wheel tree," Craig said, with a hint of sadness in his voice. But as far as last hurrahs go, it sure is a doozy.

Mr. Maasdam's sculpture is located 3 miles south of exit 179 on I–80. Head south on County Road T38 to Bethel Cemetery. Turn right at the cemetery and head west. You'll see the sculpture right ahead. There's a small parking area for visitors by the picnic table. The family offers tours of Leonard's sorghum mill down the road in September. Call (614) 594–4376 for information.

ADMIT IT, CLINT COULD MAKE YOU FEEL ADULTEROUS, TOO
Winterset

C lint Eastwood had a hard time finding just the right house for his film adaptation of James Waller's 1992 book *Bridges of Madison County*. First there was the challenge of locating a farmhouse in Madison County that was as romantically rural as the book. (Those of us who live in rural America know most real farmhouses don't look so much romantic as they look like places where people struggle to make a living.) Then there was the challenge of getting owners to agree to have their places used as a backdrop for a film about an Iowa farm wife's affair. The owners of the first farm the producers hoped to use said no. The reason? They didn't want a film depicting adultery shot on their property, with the fictitious illicit deed being done right on their living-room floor.

"I can understand that," said Gene, tour guide at the abandoned 1870 farmhouse Eastwood ended up using 15 miles north of Winterset, now called Francesca's House. "I'm kindah old-fashioned like that, too. But you know, there's one thing I can say about the movie. It didn't have any violence, it didn't have any foul language, and, in the end, Francesca did what was right—she stayed with her husband and her family."

In case you haven't read the book or seen the movie, we just gave away the ending. The movie's plot, though, is pretty simple, and pretty unapologetically romantic. Francesca (Meryl Streep) is a bored, middle-aged Italian Iowan farmwife who has just packed her two kids and husband off for a trip to the Illinois State Fair. Enter Robert Kincaid (Clint Eastwood), *National Geographic* photographer on assignment shooting Madison County's famed covered bridges. The two meet when Kincaid gets lost and asks Francesca for directions. They quickly begin

Quiet farmhouse in the country—perfect for clandestine meetings between Hollywood stars.

a passionate affair that ends with Kincaid asking Francesca to run away with him.

Gene's tour is filled with references to important scenes from the movie that were shot in various locations, from living room to kitchen to bedroom and, of course, bathtub. (Gene charmingly refers to sex scenes as "love scenes.") And he's more than generous about offering to have you sit where Clint sat (if you're a guy) or stand where Meryl stood (if you're a woman) and take your picture. He kept offering to take my picture in Clint's place, at the dining-room table, in the kitchen, outside at the windmill pump. And for some reason, I felt too self-conscious to say yes. "I'd be happy to take your picture if you want to climb into the tub," he said. (In one humdinger of a "love" scene, Francesca and Kincaid take a candlelit bath together in the family's claw-foot tub, Clint behind, Francesca in front.) When I declined the dry-bath offer (the house has never had indoor plumbing), he seemed a little shocked.

And when we went downstairs, I found out why. A whole wall in one room is filled with pictures of people in the bathtub, single men and single women, old couples, middle-aged couples, young couples, even little children, all sitting, fully clothed, in a tub where Francesca and Kincaid spent a few adulterous minutes. And something about the sweet silliness of it all made me wish I had taken Gene up on his offer.

Francesca's House is open daily, 10:00 A.M. to 5:00 P.M. from May 1 through October 18. From Winterset take U.S. Highway 169 north for 3 miles to County Road G4R and take a right. Follow County Road G4R for 13.6 miles to the marked gravel road. Turn right and go .5 mile east to the first house on the left. For more information call (515) 981–5268.

AMERICA'S SWEETEST WAR

*T*he year was 1839. An unidentified Missourian cut down three trees occupied by honey-producing bees in a small corner of a disputed border territory—now in the southern part of Van Buren County and the northern part of Missouri's Clark County—laid claim to by both Missouri and Iowa. Iowa tried the honey thief in absentia and fined him a whopping $1.50.

Missouri had become the second of the Louisiana Purchase Territories (after Louisiana) to achieve statehood in 1821, and Iowa was soon to become a state, so the question of the legal boundary between the two was a pressing issue. In 1838 a federal surveyor had laid out four possible boundaries, each of which represented a different reading of historical data (what a troublemaker). The distance between the surveyor's northernmost and southernmost boundaries was about 10 miles, creating a 10-mile strip of no-state's land all the way from the Des Moines River west to the Missouri River, totaling some 2,600 square miles.

Angry over the honey tree incident, Missouri governor Lilburn Boggs issued a proclamation stating that the surveyor's northernmost boundary was the legal state line, and in response Iowa governor Robert Lucas ordered the arrest of anyone trying to exercise authority in the disputed borderlands (what Boggs called "the seat of excitement"). At Governor Boggs's insistence Missouri's Clark County sheriff Uriah Gregory went to collect taxes in present-day Van Buren County, but Iowans in the disputed territory took him into custody and held him in Burlington. (He was allowed to

roam around town and enjoy the sights—apparently Gregory enjoyed his free Iowa vacation quite a bit.)

By December both sides began to arm (and we use the term loosely) for battle. Iowa's Governor Lucas predicted that the dispute "might ultimately lead to the effusion of blood," and called up 1,200 men. The Missourians tried to raise 2,200 militiamen, but only about half showed up—one of the "soldiers" that did make it came armed with a sausage stuffer. One militia company from Missouri's Lewis County brought six wagons of provisions, five of which were reportedly filled with booze.

Clark County sent a delegation to Iowa to work out a truce, and the militiamen spent two days camped out in the snow and the cold, drinking whiskey. In order to pass the time, they split a haunch of venison, labeled one side Governor Boggs and one side Governor Lucas, and shot each one full of holes. In Iowa the two sides agreed to allow the federal government to mediate the dispute and told their partying "troops" to go home. Ultimately, the two states came up with a brilliant solution—they'd split the disputed territory down the middle—and in 1850 they set boundary markers every 10 miles. Northern Iowans console themselves over the lost 5-mile strip of land running from one end of their state to another with a cruel joke: Handing over a part of southern Iowa to Missouri was mutually beneficial, because it raised the average IQ of both states.

You can visit the "seat of excitement" by traveling to the area between Mount Sterling and Farmington on County Road J56, south of Highway 2.

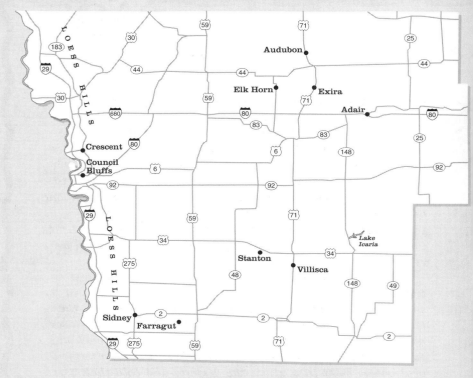

SOUTHWEST

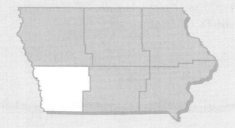

SOUTHWEST

A ROBBED TRAIN AND A SMILING TOWER
Adair

Adair's most visible landmark is its water tower, a yellow
beacon painted with a simple smiling face that's easily
seen from I–80. Its other landmark requires you exit the interstate and keep your eyes peeled for a roadside gravel loop,
which serves as the turnoff for a locomotive wheel bearing a
plaque that reads, SITE OF THE FIRST TRAIN ROBBERY IN THE WEST,
COMMITTED BY THE NOTORIOUS JESSE JAMES AND HIS GANG OF OUTLAWS
JULY 21, 1873. Town literature also calls it the world's first robbery of a moving train.

Hollywood would have you think differently about that last
claim. Michael Crichton's *The Great Train Robbery* was pur-
ported to be based on a true story about the world's first robbery of a moving train—in England in 1855. And the folks in
Verdi, Nevada, say they had a train robbery there back in 1870,
before Adair's and even farther west.

Regardless, there definitely was a train robbery here in
1873, and to clarify, the train wasn't moving while it was
robbed. The James Gang derailed the train, killing two people
and injuring several others. Then two men (believed to be Jesse
and Frank James) hopped onboard the train, forced the guard
to open the safe, and found $2,000, a full $73,000 short of
what they were expecting. They gathered another $1,000 from
passengers' pockets and then escaped.

The site of Jesse James's first train robbery in the West.
Photo: Clint Buckner

At present, the site holds the wheel and plaque as well as a few feet of the original train tracks. From it you can see the town's other claim to fame, the smiley-face water tower—less historically significant, but definitely more straightforward and cheerful.

To get to the Jesse James train-robbery site, take exit 75 off I–80 and turn on County Road G30. You'll see it on the left. For more information contact the Adair County Conservation Board at (641) 743–6450.

No (Small) Bull
Audubon

Y ou can see the bull from the highway. He's a giant Hereford with a giant set of baby-blue eyes, a giant set of horns, and a giant set of, well, those reproductive components that separate the bulls from the cows.

Albert (as the bull is named), stands 30 feet tall, has a horn span of 15 feet and weighs forty-five tons. A promotion for Audubon's beef industry, he is the world's largest bull.

By the looks of things, this bull should have courage to spare.
Photo: Berit Thorkelson

Albert's story springs from another industry promotion called Operation T-Bone, started in 1951. During the annual shipment of Audubon-area cattle to Chicago, shippers and local businessmen rode along in the train's drafty caboose—except for banker Albert Kruse, who said he'd refrain from the trip to the big city until there was a more comfortable traveling arrangement. Albert's wishes were granted, and so Operation T-Bone was born as a weeklong celebration culminating in the trip to Chicago, with the cattle in the cattle cars and the shippers and businessmen like Albert partying in style in a Pullman car. At present, Operation T-Bone is a one-day September festival with crafts and entertainment.

The big bull, erected in 1963, was named for this comfort-seeking businessman. The Jaycees took on the project, and raised about $30,000 to fund it. His steel frame, made from salvaged Iowa windmills, is covered in wire mesh, which is covered in three coats of concrete, which is covered in cement (for texture), which is covered in about 650 pounds of paint. Albert is promoted as being "authentic right down to his toenails," and this brave and extremely detailed dedication to physical authenticity is certainly difficult to miss.

Albert the Bull is located off U.S. Highway 71 at the south edge of Audubon. For more information call the Audubon Chamber of Commerce at (712) 563-3780.

AN ELDERLY DQ
Council Bluffs

I 'd run things differently if I owned it," said Jennifer, employee at the oldest Dairy Queen in the world, located right downtown in Council Bluffs. (Names have been changed to prevent ice-cream-store friction.) "First of all, there's no sign

This DQ is so old it doesn't have chocolate.

out front. I'd have a sign out front saying it was the oldest Dairy Queen."

She had a point there. The Dairy Queen looked old, but it certainly didn't jump out and say, "Oldest Dairy Queen in the Entire World." So what else would she do? "I'd have something to give people, you know, shirts or hats. The only thing I have now to give you is a receipt—it says 'America's Oldest Dairy Queen' at the top."

America's first Dairy Queen was opened in Moline on June 22, 1940, and, nine stores later, Council Bluff's Dairy Queen at Seventeenth and Broadway was opened for business on May 13, 1947. Those first nine stores have all gone bust, leaving the Council Bluffs Broadway DQ the oldest in the nation.

As some of us know, as we get older, we tend to lose a step or two. The DQ on Broadway has, unfortunately, lost its chocolate. That's right, the oldest Dairy Queen in the country serves only vanilla, and if you're really craving chocolate, you've got to head to the other DQ down the street. Simple enough, right? Well, tell that to the couple that phoned the police when they found out the girl behind the counter couldn't give them chocolate. "She kept saying, 'I'm sorry, we don't have chocolate,' and the customers kept saying they were going to call the police. So finally they called the police." And did the police issue DQ a citation? Something about serving up cones within city limits with only one flavor choice? Nope. "The officer came and he listened to the couple's story and he said, 'Why don't you just go to the other Dairy Queen?'" Another customer served; another case solved.

The oldest DQ in the country is at the corner of Seventeenth and West Broadway in Council Bluffs.

S O   W H E R E   A R E   A L L   T H E   S Q U I R R E L S ?
C o u n c i l   B l u f f s

B uilt in 1885, Council Bluffs' Squirrel Cage Jail, a three-story rotating cell drum inside a cage with only one opening per floor, was hailed as an improvement over other jails of the period. And that thought will make you even more terrified if you choose to visit.

Here's a more detailed description of how it works. The central drum is composed of three floors of circular cellblocks (or cell circles?), each divided into ten pie-shaped cells. When the jailer wished to gain access to one of the prisoners, he merely rotated the drum so that the cell door lined up with the opening. All the prisoners took a ride round the circle, then, so that one could be let out. (At least they got a change of direction, if not of scenery, once in a while.)

Of course, all that squirrel-cage convenience came with a price tag. The total cost of the building was about $30,000, but only $8,000 of it went to the exterior structure. The rest covered the cost of the rotary unit—the drum, the cage, and the massive gears—that spun the prisoners, lazy-Susan style, at least a couple of times a day.

William H. Brown and Benjamin F. Bough, the inventors of the contraption, said their goal was to provide "maximum security with minimum jailer attention." But in the end, it was the minimum inmate safety that forced Council Bluffs to close the jail because in the event of a fire or other emergency, only three men at a time could be released from their cells.

The Squirrel Cage Jail is located downtown in Council Bluffs at 226 Pearl Street, right next to the railroad museum. Call (712) 323–2509 for information.

L E A R N M O R E T H A N Y O U E V E R W A N T E D T O K N O W A B O U T L A W N M O W E R S
C r e s c e n t

I t's like porno for pack rats, grandpa's garage gone wild, with buckets of nails, an outhouse, birdcages, kerosene lamps, chainsaws. The list goes on and on, and at the base of it all are the lawnmowers, about 250 of them, the result of Fred Archer's forty-plus-year career as a lawnmower repairman. He calls it his menagerie, "a little bit of everything, but not much of anything," that is, except lawnmowers.

Fred also calls it Archer Engines of Yesteryear: Crescent Lawnmower Museum. The museum occupies a 24-by-70-foot shed and an area at least as large behind Fred's double-wide trailer (which serves as both his living quarters and an antiques store). Without Fred one might think this amassment

Old lawn mowers put out to pasture.
Photo: Berit Thorkelson

of machine after rusty machine a lawnmower graveyard. With
Fred, however, his backyard is transformed into a museum.
This curator's enthusiasm is certain to overshadow that of any
visitor, but it doesn't matter if you care. What makes this place
great is that he does.

   "That there," he says, pointing at a chunk of metal with
other chunks of metal sticking out of it, "Jacobson greens
mower originally came out with a wooden handle, patented in
1923." Then there're the ones discontinued following OSHA
regulations, the one with the engine inside the wheel, the one
that floats on air. They have come from all over the place—
customers, auctions, donations from people who've somehow

heard about Fred's passion—and most don't run (for lack of time rather than the curator's ability to revive). Despite the sheer volume Fred remembers the story behind nearly every darn one of them.

He'll tell you those stories during a personal museum tour, which can last as long as you have time for (Fred recommends you set aside a couple of hours). Expect an unstructured experience. He'll talk about whatever catches your (or his) eye, randomly connecting gas cans, hoods, and such to their rightful owners along the way.

And about the absence of Fred's right-hand pointer finger: not the result of a lawnmower accident. Working in a factory about forty-five years ago, someone turned on a machine that took this digit. Fred had to find another line of work and stumbled across lawnmower repair. And the rest, as they say, sits behind his double-wide.

Archer Engines of Yesteryear is located on the north edge of Crescent, east of Highway 183 on Riordon Street (it's not marked as such, so look for the museum's sign). Take exit 61 off Interstate 29/680. Admission is charged. Hours are officially from 10:00 A.M. to 4:30 P.M. Monday through Saturday, May through September, and other times by appointment. It's recommended that you call ahead, though: (712) 545-3791.

M I L L   Y O U R   F L O U R   T H E   D A N I S H   W A Y
E l k   H o r n

The area around Elk Horn and Kimballton was settled by Danish immigrants, and a fair majority of the people who live here now are their descendants, which makes present-day Elk Horn the largest rural Danish settlement in the United States.

Your number one source for Danish flour in the Midwest.

A lot of people have miniature windmills in their gardens, but one Elk Horn Dane, Harvey Sornson, was a bit more ambitious. When he learned that many Danish windmills were at risk of being lost to decay and neglect, he decided to try to raise enough money to dismantle a windmill in Denmark, ship it to Iowa, and then rebuild it in Elk Horn. What was first called a "crazy idea" became a rallying point for the town. Within days the town had raised $30,000, and the project was underway.

The Danish carpenter who dismantled the windmill came up with an ingenious way of aiding the Elk Horners in their rebuilding project: He numbered each beam from the windmill, created a perfect replica 6 feet tall, with correspondingly numbered beams, of course, and shipped both the dismantled mill and the model to America. "All we had to do was put the pieces of the puzzle back into the right spots," one volunteer is reported to have said.

The windmill is now the only authentic operating Danish windmill in America, and it'll probably remain the one and only. Denmark passed a law shortly after the Elk Horn windmill emigrated to America declaring it illegal to ship windmills out of the country. The mill is an official Iowa Welcome Center, and visitors can climb to the top of the mill, see the 2,000-pound grinding stones, and watch the blades turn on a windy day. And if the Dutch flour ground down at Pella's famous windmill doesn't suit your fancy, you can get your Danish flour here.

Take I–80, exit 54, and head 6 miles north. Elk Horn is at the intersection of Highway 173 and F58. The windmill is right in the center of town, and you really can't miss it. Trust us. For more information call (712) 764–7472.

A L o n g - A b a n d o n e d   F a r m   I m p l e m e n t
E x t r a

Picture, if you will, this legend: It starts with an Iowa farmer plowing his field in the early 1860s. No one knows this farmer's name, by the way, so let's call him Chet. So Chet's going about his business, using mules hooked up to a steel plow, when a bunch of Union soldiers come marching by. Remember, this is the early 1860s, so the Civil War is in full

The lesson here? Don't leave good farm implements
near trees for longer than a decade or two.
Photo: Clint Buckner

swing. Reportedly, these soldiers were on their way to battle, and being that there were no Civil War battles fought on Iowa soil, they had a lot of marching ahead of them. Chet sees these soldiers, and he is inspired. Either inspired or really tired of plowing. Either way, Chet unhitches his mules, rests his plow against a teeny burr-oak sapling, and steps in line with the soldiers. He never returns.

This is the story, anyway, and it leaves one with many questions. Wasn't Chet's family worried sick about him? I mean, here he is out plowing, and then he just disappears into thin air. Maybe he wrote once he got to wherever it was the soldiers were going. He must have; otherwise how would we now know the specifics behind his disappearance? Or was there a nosy neighbor who saw the whole thing? Did Chet grow to regret his choice, or was he totally confident in abandoning his farm and plowing duties? And who took over those duties? He'd obviously made no arrangements since this was such a spur-of-the-moment deal. And what about the mules? Did they know their way back to the barn?

"How about the plow?" you ask. "What happened to Chet's trusty plow?" That, I'm happy to report, is about all we do know about Chet's situation. Nothing happened to his plow. It's still there, and the teeny oak has grown mightily around it. All that's visible is a bit of the blade sticking out of one side and a bit of the handle sticking out the other. And the tree is huge. Nearly 100 feet tall. It sits on the edge of five-acre Plow in the Oak Park just outside of Exira. There's a picnic shelter nearby as well as a grill and bathroom facilities. The park is surrounded by cornfields, cornfields that could have been Chet's had he stuck around.

To get to Plow in the Oak Park from Des Moines, take I–80 west to US 71 north. You'll see it on the left side before you hit Exira.

A Naval Town amid Oceans of Farmland
Farragut

The town is named for a naval hero, the main street is named for his flagship vessel, the high-school nickname is "the Admirals," and local businesses play on the theme with blue-and-white paint jobs and names like "the Hair Dock." But besides the Nishnabotna River, which winds just outside of the

"But officer, the sign told me to drive this way."

Photo: Berit Thorkelson

town, there isn't a large body of water near this tiny agricultural town.

"There are anchors all over the place, and there isn't water anywhere," local farmer and poet Michael Carey good-humoredly points out. "Plus, you're going about 60 and come into town and slow down to 25 at the sign that says, DAMN THE TORPEDOES! FULL STEAM AHEAD!

Michael's referring to Farragut's town billboard, which features the most famous quote from its namesake's illustrious naval career. Farragut was the navy's first admiral and a Civil War hero, most notably for his successful capture of Mobile Bay, the Confederate's last significant port city. During this capture Admiral Farragut lashed himself to his mainsail to see over the mine (a.k.a. torpedo) smoke and called out, "Damn the torpedoes! Go ahead. Four bells!" (The quote has since been translated out of Navalese for poetic effect.)

The town's first name, in 1870, was actually Lowland, then Lawrence, but the area's first few settlers still weren't happy. One of those settlers was Major U.D. Coy, who had fought in the Black Hawk and Mexican Wars. (He also enlisted in the Civil War with his eldest son but was sent home because of his age.) Though other residents suggested Coyville, Major Coy demurred, suggesting they instead go with Farragut, a man U.D. admired. The others agreed, and in 1872 the name became official.

Every single street in town is named in connection to Admiral Farragut. Union-supporting politicians Clay and Webster each have a street, as do Civil War naval heroes Worden and Foote. Others are named after crucial Confederate forts that the admiral captured, his ships, and the president who started the American navy (Washington).

Even the newest street in town, Cushing, is named for a Civil War commander whom Farragut admired. Apparently even recent-day residents agree with the founders' sentiments: Damn the lack of water. A naval theme it is!

Farragut is located in the southwestern corner of Iowa, south of Highway 2 between U.S. Highways 275 and 59.

DIRT OF A DIFFERENT COLOR IN
RODEOTOWN
Sidney

Somehow it makes sense that a collection of dirt from around the world would find a home in Rodeotown USA. After all, dirt is a big part of rodeos, maybe even third on the list of importance, right after the horses and the cowpokes. And who knew that Rodeotown USA, was right here in Iowa? One might guess it to be in Texas, or Montana, possibly even one of the Dakotas. But here it is in Sidney, said to have one of the biggest rodeos in the country, nestled into the rolling pastoral farmland of southwestern Iowa.

Buildings in downtown Sidney play off its western moniker with weathered-wood siding and beams. One such facade gives way to the Fremont County Historical Museum, a former mechanic's garage that now preserves the past. The dirt is in the museum's back room, right by the old garage door. There are two racks: one for American dirt and another for imported dirt. The 159 specimens are kept in tiny glass jars, once used for sampling cream, affixed with typed labels proclaiming the dirt's origin. All were gathered by or gifted to Uva Turnbull, a Freemont County resident who passed away in 1970.

"When the museum first wanted to accept the donation, I thought they were crazy," said Evelyn Birkby, a local author, columnist, and museum tour guide. But Evelyn changed her tune once she saw how much visitors loved the stuff. They're encouraged to hold the glass jars for up-close views of the dirt: the fine, sparkling black sand from Hawaii; the dusty, light-brown powder from North Africa; the coarse, saltlike grains from Florida; the chunky, orange-red clumps from Korea.

There's lots of dirt on them there shelves!
Photo: Berit Thorkelson

A sheet of paper by the exhibit states that the dirt "shows that no matter where a person might live, even simple cream jars and scoops of soil can transport a person into far places and into a deeper appreciation of the lands and history of our world."

It may also show that 159 bottles of just about anything can be kinda cool to look at. The Fremont County Historical Museum is located in downtown Sidney (intersection of Highway 2 and US 275) at 801 Indiana Avenue on the east side of Courthouse Square. It's open from 1:00 to 4:00 P.M. on summer Sundays, with special hours over Memorial Day weekend and Rodeo Week, and by appointment. Call (712) 374–2335 or (712) 374–2320.

WHERE WHITE IS A WAY OF LIFE
Stanton

Nearly all the houses in Stanton are white. A few rene-
gades have stretched the theme and gone for a pale shade
of yellow or even beige. And when it comes to shutters and
trim, it's true that anything goes. But that's about as crazy as
it gets.

"I'd say it's about 90 percent white," says Don Hicks, a local
schoolteacher and coach who paints houses in town during
summer breaks. "I don't know that there was ever an ordinance
or anything, and I've never heard of any pressure. Most everybody has just followed the tradition without being forced to."

It's unclear how that tradition started. A document at the
town's Swedish Heritage and Cultural Center explains that
"long ago . . . townspeople announced plans to paint every
house in Stanton white." Even the Burlington Railroad got
onboard and painted their Stanton station white instead of the
traditional red. Travelers who saw the town from the train
nicknamed it "the Little White City."

Stanton still proudly proclaims this moniker on its town
billboard. Go ahead and make jokes. It's not like anyone's
expecting a tiny town in southwestern Iowa to be a beacon of
multiculturalism, especially given its roots. The town was
founded by a Swedish minister who offered plots only to non-
drinking, nongambling God-fearing Swedes. Today's phone
book still features a healthy number of Johnsons, Petersons,
Nelsons, and Olsons.

This last name conjures Stanton's celebrity, Virginia Christine, Mrs. Olson of Folger's Coffee fame. The town celebrates

Virginia in its two water towers—one's a coffeepot, the other a coffee cup. Both feature rosemaling and are, of course, white.

Mrs. Olson and the art of rosemaling are Swedish and therefore fit nicely with the town's roots. People tend to pin the white-house thing to these roots as well, which is ironic considering traditional Swedish houses are actually the color of the Burlington Railroad's traditional stations—red.

To get to the Little White City from Des Moines, take I–80 west to US 71. Go south on US 71 to U.S. Highway 34; then head west into Stanton.

B *ed* - *an* D - N *o* - B *reakfast* —
at Y *our* Ow *n* R *isk*
Villisca

It's the site of Iowa's worst mass murder, even though it happened back in 1912. Much of the draw is the unknown, as the murders remain unsolved. What is known: On a Sunday evening in June, someone entered the J.B. Moore home in tiny Villisca and murdered J.B., his wife, and four kids, plus two young girls who were spending the night. All the bodies were arranged neatly in their beds and covered with sheets. All the shades were drawn, and fabric hung over the doors and mirrors. The murder weapon, an axe, rested neatly inside the downstairs guest bedroom.

Darwin and Martha Linn bought the house in 1994 and began to restore it to the way it was at the time of the murders, furniture placement and all. The couple leads home tours during which they impart tons of creepy murder details and the many different (and sordid) theories as to the killer's identity. They'll top off the tour in the cemetery, if you're so inclined.

See you in the morning—we hope!
Photo: Berit Thorkelson

Since the tours began, there have also been paranormal investigators, documentarians, and a good number of tourists. A good enough number, in fact, that the Linns added special lamplit tours and overnight stays.

That's right. You can spend the night where eight people were murdered. (Don't forget that they didn't have indoor plumbing in 1912.) Some overnighters, even disbelievers, have left the house seriously shaken up, and not just because they realized how crazy it was that they decided to stay over in the first place. They say they feel things. And see things. Really.

It's worth noting that the Linns have never spent the night in the Axe Murder House. "I've never had any desire to," Darwin says, "and to be honest with you, I'm sure there's something there, and until I know what it is, I'm not staying overnight. So maybe I never will."

To get to Villisca from Des Moines, take I–80 west to US 71 south. Daytime tours of the Axe Murder House start at the Olson-Linn Museum at 323 East Fourth Street, off the town square in downtown Villisca. Admission is charged. Hours are from 9:00 A.M. to 4:00 P.M. on weekdays and from 1:00 to 4:00 P.M. on weekends. For more information or for rates and scheduling for lamplit tours and overnight stays, call (712) 826–2756 or visit www.villiscaiowa.com.

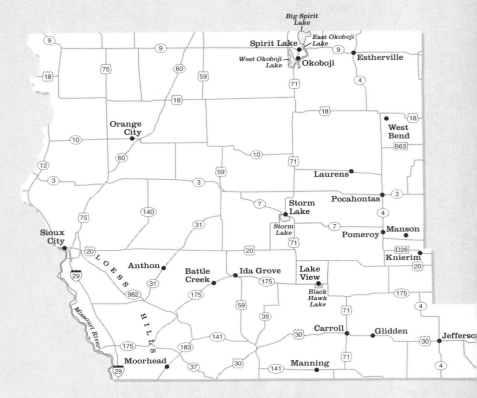

Big Spirit
Lake

Spirit Lake • East Okoboji
Lake

West Okoboji — • Okoboji
Lake

Estherville •

Orange
City •

West
Bend •

B63

Laurens •

Pocahontas •

Storm
Lake •

Storm
Lake

Pomeroy • Manson •

D26

Knierim •

Sioux
City •

L O E S S

Anthon •

H I L L S

Battle
Creek •

Ida Grove •

Lake
View •

Black
Hawk
Lake

Carroll • Glidden •

Jefferso

Moorhead •

Manning •

Missouri River

NORTHWEST

NORTHWEST

THE MAN WHO HICCUPED FOR SIXTY-NINE YEARS
Anthon

Ask ten different people how to cure hiccups, and you're likely to get ten different answers. It seems every armchair expert has his or her method of choice. Some swear by breathing into a paper bag for ten seconds; others claim holding your breath and swallowing when you feel a hiccup coming on does the trick; and a few daring, more acrobatic folk recommend taking a full glass of water, bending way forward, and drinking with head upside down, lips on the glass's far edge. Sweet-tooth hiccupers even say you should stir a teaspoonful (or tablespoonful) of sugar into a glass of water and drink it down. (It's actually pretty tasty, but it's never cured my hiccups.)

It's likely that Charles Osborne, longtime Anthon resident and lifelong hiccuper, had heard of all these hiccup cures and more. And not a single one of them worked for him. Osborne may be one of the least fortunate, semifamous Iowans in the history of the state, since he went down in the *Guinness Book of World Records* for hiccuping every one and a half seconds on average, from 1922 until his death in 1991. (If you want a little context, Charles hiccuped almost as often as his heart beat and about three times more frequently than he took breaths.) That's a total of more than 430 million hiccups over sixty-nine years. And Osborne hiccuped longer than a lot of people live.

Anthon hasn't erected any monuments to Osborne yet, though he surely deserves one for having made it through a life of hiccuping. Perhaps his constant hiccuping in a small town where people like their peace and quiet annoyed the wrong folk—everyone? Give Anthon a few more years for its frayed nerves to heal, though, and they'll form a committee, pound the pavement for donations, have a bake sale, and commission a bronze statue of Osborne with his mouth slightly open and a grimace on his poor face.

Anthon is about 20 miles southeast of Sioux City on Highway 31.

MUSEUM FULL OF NEAT JUNK
Battle Creek

What happens when an Iowa kid who likes to root around in field and stream grows older, but not necessarily up, and can no longer fit his collection of fossils, rocks, and bones into his garage?

He assembles a like-minded board of directors with names like Big R and Bomb. He gets state and local permits enabling him to gather roadkill. He calls zoos and tells them he's interested in any upcoming dead animals. He finds himself a good taxidermist, he gets himself a building, and he puts all his acquisitions inside and calls it a museum, in this case, Battle Hill Museum of Natural History in Battle Creek.

"My theory is that John Q. Public and family don't sit around the breakfast table and say, 'Let's go to a museum and learn something,'" says founder and curator Dennis Laughlin, who drives a four-wheeler with a simulated reptile-skin paint job to the museum to let guests in by appointment. "You go to

A museum for the kid in you.
Photo: Clint Buckner

see a lot of neat junk, and if you learn something in the process, great."

This is not to imply that the museum houses just a bunch of junk. Dennis has acquired quite an assemblage of interesting stuff since opening museum doors in 1990, so much so that he's added two more buildings, turned the garage into a showroom, and even turned the basement into a cave ("all it is is some chicken wire, newspaper, aluminum, two-by-fours and cardboard"). The place is stuffed with rocks, geodes, fossils, artifacts, antlers, an eagle, a black bear, ancient bison skulls, a two-headed calf, a 12,000-pound African elephant skeleton, a snow leopard, a Bengal tiger and more—much, much more.

There's a moose in the museum that gets a lot of attention, since Iowans were calling in sightings of the great animal to news stations back in 1989 until a poacher shot the thing. Parts of the moose were reportedly fed to people at a local shelter before its head found a home, amid much controversy, at Battle Hill Museum.

But Dennis calls the African elephant, which died in a zoo, his "grand prize." He has photos of the entire taxidermy process, from skinning to dipping parts in a peroxide-filled kiddie pool in his backyard to skeletal assembly.

"I get to build rocks, and I'd never gotten to skin an elephant before. I just like to do this," Dennis says. But it's not all about the kid in him, it's about actual kids, as school groups regularly tour the museum. "If there's a kid who likes dinosaurs, I guarantee he'll go home with a dinosaur bone," Dennis says. "When you get a kid in here that's genuinely interested, that's as good as it gets."

The Battle Hill Museum of Natural History is on Highway 175 on the northeast side of Battle Creek. It's open by appointment. Call (712) 365–4414 or visit www.pionet.net/~bhmuseum.

No More War! (There's No Place to Put Another Monument)
Carroll

The town of Carroll put its patriotism where its cemetery is and erected a monument that pays tribute to the soldiers who have fought and served honorably in every United States war, at least, every United States war up until the war on terror.

As of right now, they've got a circle of 7-by-7-foot square fieldstone monuments commemorating the Spanish American War, World War I, World War II, the Korean War, the Vietnam War, and the Persian Gulf War, all arranged around a Civil War obelisk. At the top of each stone is an engraving of images emblematic of the war; the Vietnam monument, for example, has soldiers marching through grass, a couple of "Hueys" flying overhead.

There didn't seem to be space for any more monuments, but when I asked the cemetery manager about it, he assured me there was room. "I've got space for two more," he said. When I asked him if the town was thinking of adding a monument for either the Afghanistan or Iraq war, or maybe one monument that included both, he said no one had brought it up yet. "I guess no one's thought of it. I'll have to bring it up at the next meeting," he told me. But maybe you need to wait until a war is over before building a monument.

In Carroll the monument is located in the northeast corner of the cemetery at South Grant Road and East Anthony Street, just by Quemper Field House.

Is This My Meteorite?
Estherville

On May 10, 1879, the largest meteorite known to have fallen in North America planted itself 14 feet deep on Sever Lee's farm about 3 miles north of Estherville. When Lee didn't show much interest in the rock, a group of young men hired a well digger, George Osborn, to help them raise it. It weighed 437 pounds and measured 27 x 22¾ x 15 inches. Realizing the potential value of the meteorite, the boys loaded it onto a wagon with a large sign that read, I AM THE HEAVENLY METEOR. I ARRIVED MAY 10TH AT 5 O'CLOCK. FROM WHENCE I CAME NOBODY KNOWS, BUT I AM ENROUTE FOR CHICAGO. (A surprisingly well-spoken but very enigmatic meteorite. And quite anxious to leave Iowa for the big city.)

The group didn't get too far to Chicago before they heard rumors that their ownership was being challenged, so they returned to Estherville and first buried the meteorite in Osborn's cornfield and then transferred it to one of the group member's homes. Meanwhile, Keokuk attorney Charles Birge had discovered that Sever Lee defaulted on his farm payments and, making successful claim to the land, obtained a writ of attachment to the meteorite and summarily took it from the boys. Later he sold it to the British Museum of Natural History in London for what was rumored to be a large sum of money. Poor Sever Lee didn't know what hit him or his former farm.

The meteorite that landed in Lee's field was only one of three large pieces that fell around Estherville that day. Residents were startled by a loud explosion "like the report of a cannon," the newspapers said, and then heard thunderous sounds, "what seemed to be echoes of the first shot." Witnesses

saw what appeared to be a fireball traveling across the sky
from the southeast to northwest, and two people 6 miles west
of Estherville reported seeing the meteorite split into three
pieces, with the three vapor trails making what appeared to be
a crow's foot in the sky. The two other large pieces were found
within a few miles of Lee's farm. The first, found four days
later, weighed 151 pounds and was sold to the University of
Minnesota; the second, weighing in at 106 pounds, wasn't
found until February 1890. Taking into account the more than
5,000 smaller pieces that were collected by residents—"gathering meteors" became a favorite leisure activity for Estherville
residents for a couple of years—experts estimated the
Estherville meteorite had a total weight of around 744 pounds,
making it the largest meteor in North America.

Estherville's meteorite is now housed in museums all over
the world including the National Museum of Natural History
in Paris, the Natural History Museum of Vienna, the U.S.
National Museum in Washington, the Field Museum in Chicago
(Mr. Heavenly Meteor did, in fact, make it to Chicago after all),
and the Peabody Museums at Yale, Harvard, and Amherst.
Estherville wouldn't have anything but small meteorite pebbles
and keepsakes (residents crafted larger fragments into rings)
were it not for the generosity of the University of Minnesota,
which loaned the chamber of commerce a chunk of their 151-
pound specimen for display in the town's beautifully renovated
1903 Carnegie Library. Estherville also placed a boulder with a
bronze tablet to mark the spot where the largest piece fell on
Lee's farm.

And speaking of Lee, if you're worried about what happened to poor Sever after Charles Birge took his farm and his
meteorite (he might as well have stolen his wife, too), then
worry no more. Birge deeded the farm back to Sever Lee—
minus one very large and valuable rock from outer space—a
year later.

Estherville's Carnegie Library, which contains a fragment
of the second meteorite chunk to be discovered, is located in

downtown Estherville. For more information call (712)
362–7731. You can also visit the boulder and bronze plaque,
located 2 miles north of Estherville on Highway 4, which
marks the hole (or marks a spot precisely 432 feet west of the
hole) where the 437-pound meteorite fell on Lee's farm.

A Son's Tribute Gone Awry
Glidden

Colonel Paul Tibbets, World War II B-29 bomber pilot, paid
his mother the great tribute of naming his plane after her.
What a proud moment that must have been for his mom, an
Iowa native hailing from the small town of Glidden, when she
learned that the plane that carried her son and his crew on
their perilous journeys and brought them safely home again,
mission after mission, was named in her honor. And then came
Little Boy.

On August 6, 1945, Colonel Paul Tibbets and his crew
dropped the first atomic bomb, "Little Boy," on Nagasaki. The
name of the plane that delivered the bomb, of course, was the
Enola Gay.

The Tibbets have moved away from Glidden, but the legacy
of Colonel Paul Tibbets and *Enola Gay* lives on in Glidden,
albeit in a humble form. The family donated a picture of the
Enola Gay, which now hangs in the public library.

Glidden is located on U.S. Highway 30 east of Carroll. The
Glidden Public Library is located downtown, at 131 Idaho
Street. For information call (712) 659–3781.

SMALL IOWA TOWN, BIG MEDIEVAL STYLE
Ida Grove

*B*yron Godbersen had a thing for castles. Being a millionaire, he also had the means to indulge in his fascination. We're not talking about a scale-models-in-the-basement type of indulgence, here; we're talking about full-on castles built around Byron's hometown of Ida Grove.

A newspaper housed in royal digs.
Photo: Clint Bruckner

Entering the town from the west is a surreal experience. There's the huge stone observation tower/city marker, the stone-towered suspension bridge on the local golf course, and all the castle-themed buildings connected with Midwest Industries, the manufacturing company Byron founded and one of the city's top employers. For example, armored knights stand watch at the stone gate in front of the Midwest Industries facility designed to test and display products like boat hoists. From the gate you can see eight-acre Lake LaJune, named for Byron's wife, which was once an eight-acre cornfield. On it floats a half-scale replica of the HMS *Bounty*, a late-1700s full-rigged merchant ship.

And that's not all. Byron thought the town of about 2,300 needed a second newspaper, so he started the *Ida County Courier* and designed that downtown building like a castle, too. He also built the aptly named Skate Palace, with its flag-topped turrets and wood-heavy medieval interior. Other local non-Byron businesses, like Kastle Kones, play off the established theme.

Byron was one of few people whose home was, literally, his castle, a far cry from the farmhouse in which he grew up. (Byron passed away in May of 2003, but LaJune still lives there.) Byron's attempt to make farm life easier led to his fortune. Midwest Industries' first product was a hydraulic hoist for farm wagons and things only grew from there. Byron remains Iowa's most prolific inventor with more than 50 patents to his name.

The question remains: Why castles? The best answer I could dig up was that on a trip to Europe, Byron was struck by the stone structures he saw. He returned to Iowa and, bit by bit, began to turn Ida Grove into a kind of medieval Iowan Mayberry, a place where castles meet Kum and Go.

From Sioux City head east on U.S. Highway 20, then south on U.S. Highway 59 into Ida Grove. For more information contact the Ida Grove Chamber of Commerce at (712) 364–3404 or visit www.idagrovechamber.com.

Lighthouse on the Prairie
Jefferson

*B*uilt in the sixties, Jefferson's bell tower on the square is flagrantly modern, if you know what we mean. And though it strikes a discordant note at first glance—a 120-foot-tall modern bell tower in the middle of an Iowa farm town—the more you look at, the more it grows on you. Think of it as a lighthouse overlooking a sea of prairie. And then, when the electronic carillon begins to play "America the Beautiful," (of course, the carillon is electronic in a 1960s bell tower), you just might fall in love.

You can take a tour and look out on beautiful America from the observation deck, which sits ten stories high above the town. The carillon chimes every quarter hour, but it also plays religious and patriotic music at 11:00 A.M., 2:00 P.M., and 5:00 P.M. daily.

Jefferson is also home to a telephone museum. You can trace the evolution of the phone from the hand-crank jobbies you see in movies (with the mouthpiece on the phone box) to the more modern models you're familiar with. If you're the type who not only hates cell phones but gets shivers when you feel rotary-phone plastic wrapped tightly around your index finger, then this museum will send you into ecstasies of nostalgia.

The tower is at the corner of Lincoln Way and Wilson Street in downtown Jefferson and is open Memorial Day to Labor Day, 11:00 A.M. to 4:00 P.M. daily. For information or appointment, call (515) 386–2155. The museum is located at 105 West Harrison Street and is open Monday through Friday, 9:00 A.M. to 5:00 P.M. For more information call (515) 386–4141.

A NAPOLEON-COMPLEX COUPLE
Knierim

At 4 feet 10 inches and 85 pounds and 5 feet 7 inches, 127 pounds, respectively, Bonnie Parker and Clyde Barrow made for a decidedly unimposing pair. Of course, looks can be deceiving. In a little more than two years, the couple killed a dozen people (including nine lawmen), kidnapped many others, and robbed countless small-town banks and businesses during the early 1930s.

Ian Frazier, in his book *Great Plains*, gives this description of Bonnie and Clyde: "Clyde had on his right arm the tattoo of a girl and the name 'Grace.' Bonnie had on the inside of her right thigh a tattoo of two hearts joined by an arrow, with 'Bonnie' in one heart and 'Roy' in the other. They kept a white rabbit, and took it with them on their travels. Clyde also brought along his saxophone and sheet music. Bonnie read *True Romance* magazines, painted her toenails pink, and dyed her hair red to match her hats, dresses, and shoes." According to one police investigator, Bonnie and Clyde loved to drive fast and far and "thought nothing of driving a thousand miles at a stretch." On one of these junkets in 1934 (just months before they were shot dead in a police ambush near Gibsland, Louisiana), they stopped for a brief visit in Knierim (pronounced ke-neer-em) to make a $272 withdrawal from the bank. Of course, they didn't have an account at Knierim's bank, and they completed the transaction from behind the barrel of a gun.

Now, the town of Knierim, a small group of homes beside a grain elevator, no longer has what you might think of as a downtown. The buildings are still there—hyper-plain brick structures, a couple of which have wooden false fronts that give the street a slightly western feel—but the businesses have long since gone bust. There's a building with faded hand-painted signs that say SALOON and ICE FOR SALE, but the saloon's closed, and a trailer home has been plunked down beside it. Both Jud's Grocery and the bank Bonnie and Clyde robbed, a simple square block of a brick building, have been converted into private residences.

Knierim is so small that when I asked a man who was helping a neighbor unload a refrigerator about the bank robbery, he said that his grandfather was waiting in line at the bank at the time of the holdup. "He said they were as friendly and polite as can be," he told me. And that means a lot to small town Iowans—if you're going to rob, kidnap, and kill, at least do it with a smile.

Knierim is north of US 20 at the intersection of County Roads D26 and P19. The bank is right "downtown," the farthest brick building from the railroad tracks.

A PARADE WITH REAL FLOATS
Lake View

*H*ere's a question: Why are parade floats called "floats"? After all, they don't really float; they roll. Granted, most so-called "float" makers deceptively cover the wheels of their creations so that they appear to float rather than roll down the street. But roll they do.

Enter Lake View and its lighted water-float parade to reestablish linguistic accuracy. Pam Wollesen, owner of Day Dreamers Gift and Souvenir Shop in downtown Lake View and thirty-year-veteran organizer of the town's summer water carnival, says the parade of lighted water floats "is really something else." Exactly, and that something else is a parade with honest-to-goodness floats.

The water-float parade began back in the 1950s and has since become the Black Hawk Lake Summer Water Carnival's signature event. Back then, the floats were made out of cardboard on pontoons, but after rain disintegrated the floats one year, Lake View started building them out of wood. Each float is constructed on pontoons (or a pontoon boat), fitted with a generator, and then strung with lots and lots of lights. Then, when darkness falls on Sunday night, boats tow each float in a parade around the bays and inlets of Black Hawk Lake while residents and visitors watch the procession from the shore.

Now the town contracts its floats out to one woman, who makes all fifteen to twenty in the parade. "People just don't have the time or resources to make them," Wollesen said, "so we hire out." Businesses and civic groups in town sponsor floats (or parts of floats), and residents and visitors get to sit on the shore and enjoy the parade, with floats lit up bright as Christmas trees, without ever having to smash a thumb with a hammer or step on a nail.

The Water Carnival, held the second weekend in July, also features a regular parade (with rolling floats), Saturday-night fireworks over the lake, a lip-sync contest, the Little Miss Black Hawk Pageant, and, miracle of miracles, a quiet tractor pull (it's a pedal-tractor pull). But the floats are the real crowd pleasers. "It was the only water parade in the state for a long time, but now I think they might have one somewhere out east on the Mississippi. I'm not sure, though," said Wollesen. But Lake View gets credit for having the first parade in the state with floats that really float.

Lake View is located on Black Hawk Lake at the intersection of US 71 and County Road M68. The Black Hawk Lake Summer Water Carnival is held on the second weekend of July. For more information call (712) 657–2664.

TOWER TO CESSNA 5RW3: WE HAVE A MESSAGE — FORE!
Laurens

Iowa has more golfers per capita than any other state in the union, and with so much land under cultivation, we have to get a little creative about where we play. The town of Lake View, for example, hosts the Arctic Open on the first Saturday in February, with a 9-hole course on frozen Black Hawk Lake. (Participants hate the snow traps but love the fact that the only water hazard in the area is under 9 inches of bulletproof ice.) Then there's Des Moine's Skywalk Open, an annual 18-hole minigolf tournament held in the city's 3 miles of downtown skywalks.

But the award for the most creative and potentially dangerous alternative golf space has to go to Laurens, whose Skyways Airport is both an airport and a golf course, the Laurens Country Club. The airport came first, and then the golfers planned a course around it, making the grass runway do double-duty as a fairway. It's one of only two golf-course airports in the country, with the other located in Wisconsin.

Golfers love the Laurens Country Club, not least of all because an airplane landing on the fairway offers a ready-made excuse for slicing into the rough. Club scorecards come printed with the reminder that airplanes, not golfers, have the runway right of way, and pilots don't even have to ask if they can play through. The country club does, however, ask that they circle the fairway once (and buzz the clubhouse if they feel so inclined) before landing to give golfers a chance to clear the runway.

According to course manager Carol Thomas, with a runway on the course, golfers aren't the only ones who end up in the rough. "One guy misjudged the runway and came bouncing down the rough," she said. "He ended up on the eighth green, dripping oil all over the place." She seemed so miffed by the fact that her groundskeepers had to replant the green that she didn't even say how close he came to the pin.

Laurens Skyways Airport and the Laurens Country Club are both located just west of town at 12582 Highway 10. For more information call (718) 841–2287.

THE FURRY BARN FROM ACROSS THE SEA
Manning

Not to be outdone by the Danish Elk Horners up the road (who shipped a windmill all the way from the Old Country to Iowa), the Manning Heritage Foundation received as a gift from Herr Claus Manning a 350-year-old authentic so-called German Hausbarn from the village of Offenseth in Schleswig-Holstein, Germany. (In 1991, when he made the offer of the Hausbarn, Herr Claus still had tenants in the building, according to the woman at the gift shop, so Manning had to wait a few years for the people to move out.)

The thatched Hausbarn, an American adaptation from the German "farmer's house," was common to the Schleswig-Holstein region of Germany during the seventeenth and eighteenth centuries. The Hausbarn's most unusual feature? It's designed to house both the farmer's family and his livestock. Of course, such living arrangements make for cramped and decidedly aromatic conditions. And it should go without saying that if you don't wake up early, it's hell trying to get into the bathroom.

The Hausbarn was dismantled and shipped to Iowa in 1996, groundbreaking was held in 1997, and in July 1999 master

It's a house and a barn in one! Can you say "strong household odors"?

carpenter Martin Hansen arrived from Germany to lead volunteers in the reconstruction. The steep thatched roof, which the gift-shop saleswomen assured me never leaked, is made from Baltic Sea reeds bunched tightly together and makes the whole building look kind of fuzzy at the eaves.

Hausbarn/Heritage Park Grove, as the site is called, also offers some beautiful grounds as well as a 1915 bungalow-style homestead that's being restored for use as a museum and exhibit. At press time workers were also putting the finishing touches on a German-style restaurant and conference center right beside the Hausbarn, so you can get a taste of the old country while you network, too. And a reminder: Though the Hausbarn was originally intended for livestock as well as peo-

ple, now that we have health codes and such, livestock are no
longer permitted. So just leave Bessie in the trailer.

Manning is located on Highway 141, 7 miles west of the
intersection with US 71. The Hausbarn is just east of town on
the south side of Highway 141 at the intersection with Concord
Road. For more information call (712) 655–3131.

THE DAY IOWA IGNITED
Manson

A bout seventy-four million years ago, central Iowa lay near
a shallow inland sea and had a climate similar to that of
the present-day Gulf of Mexico. (Sounds nice, doesn't it? Spring
Break Iowa 74 million B.C.!) But, unfortunately, the pleasant
subtropical environment took a cataclysmic turn for the worse.
If you think Iowa natural disasters are bad these days—think
back to the Great Flood of 1993, the biggest natural disaster in
United States history—you'd better brace yourself.

At some point around seventy-four million years ago (give
or take a few 100,000 years), a meteor 1 mile in diameter and
weighing ten billion tons blasted through the atmosphere and
crashed to earth—you guessed it—right in central Iowa, with
the bulls-eye directly over present-day Manson. The meteorite
penetrated about 1 mile into the earth's surface, and the shock
waves instantaneously ignited everything within a 130-mile
radius of the point of impact. In other words, most of Iowa, its
fern-rich forests, its dinosaurs, amphibians, and smaller mam-
malian inhabitants, went up in flames. Scientists speculate that
the earth and dust driven into the atmosphere blocked the sun
for months, and recent researchers theorized that the meteor
could have contributed to the extinction of dinosaurs and other
species about sixty-five million years ago.

You won't find any mile-deep craters around Manson these days, though. The Manson Crater, as it is appropriately named, has been eroded by glacial scraping and buried under 100 to 300 feet of glacial-silt deposits over the last couple of million years. (Scientist proved the existence of the crater by drilling for samples of rock and soil.) But knowing the history of Manson, or the land it now sits upon, has to make residents feel safe from a meteor impact. After all, what are the chances a 1-mile-wide meteorite will vaporize the same place twice?

Manson is located due west of Fort Dodge (North Central region) on Highway 7.

HUNDREDS OF MILES OF HILLS IN IOWA
Moorhead

S tretching for more than 200 miles north and south along the eastern edge of the Missouri floodplain, the Loess Hills are one of Iowa's most outstanding geological features. The hills were formed in much the same way snowdrifts or sand dunes are formed: by wind. During the Ice Age glaciers ground underlying rock into fine sediment called glacial flour, which was deposited on the Missouri floodplain as the glaciers melted, creating huge mudflats. When the melt waters receded, the mudflats dried, and the silt was carried by westerly winds to the east, where it was deposited over broad areas. The heavier, coarser silt deposited closest to the Missouri formed sharp, high bluffs on the western edge of the Loess Hills, whereas the lighter silt deposited on the Loess's eastern edge formed gently sloping hills.

The end result is that western Iowa, one of the flattest regions of the state, has a range of strikingly beautiful and geologically interesting hills and bluffs running along almost

A real curiosity—hills in western Iowa.

the entire length of the Missouri floodplain. Are the Loess Hills unique? Not quite, but the only other place in the world with loess hills so tall (loess, pronounced "luss," is German for loose or crumbly) is Shanxi, China.

The hills' unique geology is evident even to the untrained eye. Sharp bluffs, irregular peaks and saddles, deep gullies, and staircaselike features on some hillsides are all testament to the way the hills were formed and the way they're now eroding. (The hillside staircases, called cat steps, are actually the result of slipping soil.) Unfortunately, the Loess Hills are incredibly fragile. Since the fine silt deposits don't contain any clay, the material that normally binds wet soil together, the Loess Hills have one of the highest erosion rates in the United States.

Efforts are underway to protect the Loess Hills from man-made sources of erosion, not only to preserve the hills in their own right but to hold onto one of the strongest pieces of evidence we have to prove to out-of-staters that Iowa is most certainly not flat.

The Loess Hills stretch along almost the entire western Iowa border, with hiking, camping, and scenic drives throughout. For information visit the Loess Hills Hospitality Association Visitor's Center and Gift shop in downtown Moorhead on Highway 183. Open daily from 9:00 A.M. to 4:30 P.M. in summer and from 10:00 A.M. to 4:30 P.M. in winter. For more information call (712) 886–5441.

A SUBTLE CELEBRATION OF A NOT-SO-SUBTLE WEED
Moorhead

Sometimes it's Crabgrass Days, and other times it's more of a Crabgrass Day, or Crabgrass Afternoon, even Crabgrass Morning. And to be honest, except for the name, there's really nothing about Moorhead's festival that has anything to do with crabgrass.

Shelia Lindsey at the Loess Hills Hospitality Association explains that when the festival in this town of about 250 started in the 1990s, people just wanted something to do in September. Because the time they chose to schedule an excuse to hang out coincided with the time of the year when crabgrass is in full bloom, the community decided to name the festival for the weed. While they were at it, they declared themselves the Crabgrass Capital of Iowa.

That first year was the biggest, and there was even a contest for the largest blade of crabgrass, held in the town park.

Things have calmed down significantly since that wild and crazy opener.

"Now it's a relaxed day in the park for the residents of the city, an old-fashioned community get-together," Shelia says. "Some are bigger than others. There may be a potluck meal in the evening, a talent show, a dance, a cakewalk. Sometimes we have a parade. It just depends on which volunteers are active at the time and how the spirit moves them."

The year I spoke to Shelia, the festival was scheduled to consist of a community church service where residents would gather as one regardless of religious affiliation followed by a pancake feed. When I pressed her about the absence of anything related to the festival's namesake, she said it might make a subtle appearance. "We'll have wildflowers at the church service," she told me. "We'll probably have a few sprigs of crabgrass tucked in there."

Crabgrass Days (or Day) is usually held on the third weekend in September in Moorhead, located on Highway 183 north of Council Bluffs. For more information call the Loess Hills Hospitality Association at (712) 886–5441.

HIGHER LEARNING OKOBOJI STYLE
Okoboji

Even though it has more square miles of lake, more beaches, more restaurants, and way more beachfront rental property than any university in the country, the University of Okoboji (U of O) hasn't ever made the list of the ten-most-beautiful college campuses in America. Though the hundreds of thousands of alumni of the university might think the situation scandalous, they really don't have a very compelling argument for Okoboji's inclusion on the list. After all, the University of Okoboji isn't an accredited, degree-granting institution, doesn't award its professors tenure (or even have professors), doesn't offer a single course in the hard sciences (or in the soft sciences, the humanities, medicine, engineering, or law for that matter), and—are you ready for this shocker?— doesn't field a single sports team. (Are we still in Iowa?)

Still, Okoboji's merchandising machine must be stuck in overdrive, because it's hard to go anywhere in Iowa without seeing U of O hats, pennants, sweatshirts, jackets, and those stickers people place in the back windows of their cars. The vacation-destination joke started about thirty years ago when Herman Richter and his brother Emil—owners of the Three Sons clothing store in Milford—began calling their Iowa Great Lakes playground "The University of Okoboji." They and a group of their sports-playing friends took to wearing University of Okoboji T-shirts, and soon the U of O crest started appearing on just about anything and everything visitors would buy.

In 1988 community leaders decided to establish a foundation in support of projects that improve the quality of life in the Iowa Great Lakes region, and the University of Okoboji generously offered the use of its name. Now, the University of Okoboji and the foundation together play host to a yearly calendar of events that's almost as full as a real university's. There's the University of Okoboji Winter Games in late January (the broom-hockey tournament is a favorite), the University of Okoboji soccer and rugby tournaments, a U of O marathon, and the annual U of O homecoming weekend in July, with a parade, triathlon, and cleanup drive, but, alas, no football game. And that's just the beginning.

And the best thing is, although Okoboji is a university town, there's no town/gown tensions, for two reasons: All the residents are University of Okoboji students by default, and at the University of Okoboji, no one wears gowns; it's strictly a swimsuit crowd.

The Iowa Great Lakes region is located north of Spencer at the intersection of US 71 and Highway 9. For more information about University of Okoboji events, call (800) 270–2574 or visit www.vacationokoboji.com. To buy University of Okoboji apparel, visit Three Sons in Milford's financial district or call (712) 338–2424. They also have a Web site where you can buy merchandise: www.threesons.com.

A WIND-POWERED PHONE BOOTH
Orange City

Okay, so the small windmill at the corner of Central Avenue and West First Street in downtown Orange City isn't really operational—the blades don't power anything, nor do they rotate a single inch, even in a good stiff prairie wind—but what the windmill lacks in authenticity it surely makes up for in originality. It may be the only pay-phone-booth windmill in the country, maybe even the world.

Orange City is yet another small Iowa town with a strong Dutch heritage, and they've got the big windmill to prove it. You can find it out on Highway 10 just east of town, a 75-foot-tall, 14-ton windmill housing the chamber of commerce and visitor center. Orange City's downtown businesses also feature false decorative fronts painted in cheery colors to give the place a pseudo-Dutch feel, the streets are lined with tulips in spring and marigolds in summer, and the high-school marching band is reported to perform in Dutch wooden shoes on special occasions (sounds downright painful).

But the most original expression of Dutch heritage in town is the windmill phone booth. Sure, phone booths have become passé and a bit neglected with the invention and meteoric rise of the cell phone, but Orange City may have found a way to keep humble pay phones alive. Turn them into Dutch windmills, and people may dig in their pockets for loose change to call home just for the sheer novelty of it all.

Orange City's windmill phone booth is located downtown, at the corner of Central Avenue and West First Street. For more information about events in Orange City, call the Chamber of Commerce at (712) 707–4510.

A B i g A m e r i c a n I n d i a n W e l c o m e
P o c a h o n t a s

The 25-foot-tall statue of Pocahontas on the outskirts of the city of Pocahontas in the county of Pocahontas certainly commands attention.

No matter what you think of her appearance, you must admit she serves her purpose. Senator Albert Shaw and his son, Frank, saw giant statues of fish and Paul Bunyan in Minnesota and thought Pocahontas, too, should have such a community symbol. What better symbol for the community of Pocahontas than its namesake Pocahontas? (For those of you who don't recall your elementary-school history classes, Pocahontas was the American Indian Princess credited for saving the life of Captain John Smith, the English leader of the Jamestown, Virginia, colonists back in the early 1600s.)

In 1953 Frank hired the man behind the giant muskie statue in Minnesota to design *Miss Pocahontas*. He then contracted his friend and fellow Poky (as town residents call themselves) Marcell Moritz to build her. During his spare time over the course of two years, Marcell crafted Pocahontas out of wood, steel, and cement. He finished in 1956. She has stood

This Indian princess would dominate in the WNBA.
Photo: Clint Buckner

ever since, on Highway 3 just east of the city, serving as a landmark and greeting visitors headed into town or on their way to or from nearby vacation destinations.

Whether for reasons of beauty or gender ambiguity, the statue is nothing if not memorable. "When you're a kid growing up, you think it's pretty cool. Then you get older and realize it's just not that attractive," said one former Pocahontas resident who wishes to remain nameless. "But it is a great conversation starter, something the town is easily recognized for. You go somewhere and people say, 'Oh, Pocahontas, I've been there. That town with the Indian.'"

A L O N G , S T R A N G E T R I P
P o m e r o y

The dancing bears on the sign outside Byron's are like Deadhead code. To the casual observer, they are, at best, a questionably cutesy choice for a place where people go to knock 'em back. To a Grateful Dead fan, they are a total trip in tiny Pomeroy, a guarantee that someone nearby is ready to listen to your stories about killer bootlegs and the Jerry Days.

The place first stands out from Pomeroy's 1-block downtown because it's occupied—even the town hall has moved to the local minimall. I ran across it in on a random Sunday, when owner Byron Stuart was getting ready for business. Nearly every square inch of the place was packed with Dead memorabilia, from posters and T-shirts to stuffed bears and stickers. Byron was wearing a tie-dyed T-shirt and had Dead tunes playing in the background. He told me that the motif, made up of gifts and items from his personal collection, was an accident. "It was just a generic bar, and I wasn't going to turn it into a Grateful Dead bar, but on the first day some girls

A place for the tie-dye and dreads set.
Photo: Clint Buckner

brought in a framed T-shirt of Jerry Garcia, and it set the
mood," he says.

Truth be told, Byron was a Deadhead long before the gift.
He first saw the Dead in Des Moines in 1972, and he was
hooked. The other 781 residents of Pomeroy don't necessarily
share Byron's taste in music. "When I moved back here, nobody
had heard of the Grateful Dead," Byron says. "Now they know
the name, but maybe think it's a devil-worshiper band."

Local regulars may or may not stick around on live-music nights to hear the hippie jam bands, acoustic folk rockers, and old-school biggies Byron books from both the surrounding regions and around the country. (Canned Heat once made the trek and loved it—said it was like playing in Byron's living room.) Byron relies heavily on word of mouth as a promotional tool. Sometimes this packs 'em in, mostly from a 40-mile radius; other times it doesn't. Either way, he gets his live-music fix without having to drive for hours to a bigger city.

And then Byron's goes back to being your average small-town bar that happens to be drenched in Grateful Dead memorabilia. Byron has kindly stocked the jukebox with a wide range of music for his solid base of regulars. Every once in a while a Dead tune comes on, and when Byron catches a local compulsively tappin' his toes, he smiles.

Byron's is located at 112 Main Street. For more information call (712) 468–2372 or visit www.palmerwebservices.com/byron's.

Monument to a Fallen Sergeant
Sioux City

In 1803 Meriwether Lewis and William Clark accepted orders from Thomas Jefferson to explore the newly acquired Louisiana Purchase and seek an all-water route to the Pacific. On May 14, 1804, the explorers headed up the Missouri; they reached the Pacific in November 1805, and they returned to St. Louis on September 23, 1806.

Of course, quite a bit happened in between. Lewis and Clark's expedition journal entry for Monday, August 20, 1804, just three months into the journey, describes the death and burial of one Sergeant Floyd, the only member of the party to die on the two-year, four-month, nine-day, 8,000-plus-mile jour-

A memorial to a man whose luck ran out in Iowa.

ney. Of all the future states in which the explorer could have bit it, he chose Iowa, and of that we can be proud.

"We buried him at the top of a high round hill," the journal reads, "overlooking the river and country for a great distance situated just below a small river without a name to which we name and call Floyd's River, the bluff Sgt. Floyd's Bluff." The round hill, the bluff, the river, and the great view are all still there, just south of Sioux City. And to honor the fallen sergeant and his great instincts about final resting places, the city built a 100-foot-tall, 717-ton white sandstone obelisk on the hill to mark his grave site. The bluff offers a panoramic view of the Missouri River and Nebraska to the west.

So how did Sergeant Floyd die? Was he killed while protecting Sacagawea from a hostile Indian raid? Was he braving rapids or scaling a cliff or wrestling a bear? Unfortunately, his death was decidedly undramatic. Modern medical authorities now believe Floyd's death was caused by complications arising from appendicitis, a condition that had no cure at the time except leeches, and those were awaiting FDA approval (hungrily we might add).

The journal entry for the day of Floyd's death concludes, "We returned to the boat and proceeded to the mouth of little river, 30 yards wide, and camped a beautiful evening." Lewis and Clark didn't seem to lose much sleep over Sergeant Floyd's death, even on the very evening they buried him. But we all know how detached explorers can be, what with their wanderlust and fear-of-intimacy issues.

The Sergeant Floyd monument is northeast of exit 143 off Interstate 29.

THREE-STORY-TALL STAINLESS-STEEL MARY AND JESUS
Sioux City

Take an abandoned Catholic boarding school on a hilltop, tear it down, add a 30-foot-tall, five-ton stainless-steel statue of Mother Mary, a 33-foot-tall stainless-steel statue of Jesus, lots of landscaped gardens, and a building housing a hand-carved, life-sized wooden sculpture of the Last Supper, and what do you have? Well, we're not quite sure, but it's called Trinity Heights.

The Virgin Mary looking radiant.

Queen of Peace Inc., a nonprofit group, has spent more than $1 million erecting the towering statues and developing the fifty-three-acre site for visitors. The project began with sculptor Dale Lamhere's statue of the Immaculate Heart of Mary Queen of Peace, set in place on December 16, 1992. The statue of Jesus was erected six years later, on June 9, 1998. Made from unadorned, unpainted stainless steel, with hands and faces as gray as their robes, the sculptures appear strangely modern.

The site also contains a gift shop which sells religious books, videos, and paraphernalia, and the Saint Joseph Center Museum, which houses the life-sized Last Supper carving as well as artifacts from the Trinity Schools, which once stood on the grounds. A self-taught sculptor, Jerry Traufler spent seven years carving his Last Supper by mallet and chisel. Traufler used Da Vinci's painting *The Last Supper* as his model, but instead of cribbing the disciples' faces from the master, he used models from his hometown of Le Mars, including his own wife, stand-in for the disciple John, seated to the right of Christ. (There's a picture along the back wall with the Le Mars models standing over the shoulders of their respective disciple doubles.)

"Those are some big chunks of wood," my tour guide said. "Each one weighed somewhere between 200 and 300 pounds, without appendages. The hands and feet and the sandals—he made those separately so he could remove 'em. That way he could move the disciples around in his shop and not knock all the digits off their little hands." And as everyone knows, when you're working with disciples, it's important to keep all digits intact, especially when one of them happens to be your wife.

Trinity Heights, located at the corner of Thirty-third Street and Floyd Avenue, is open April through October, 10:00 A.M. to 9:00 P.M., and November through March, 10:00 A.M. to 4:00 P.M. From I-29, take the Stockyards exit (147A) to Floyd Boulevard. Travel north about 3 miles, and then turn west on Thirty-third Street just after Sioux Tools. For more information call (712) 239-8670.

WORLD-RECORD HOUSE BUILDER
Spirit Lake

*B*ryan Berg, famous Iowa builder, travels all over the world doing construction projects, gets paid thousands and thousands of dollars for his services, and almost always has the delicious pleasure of knocking down his pricey buildings once they're completed. Berg's demolition tool of choice? A leaf blower.

Though it may not seem possible for a simple blower to summarily take down the equivalent of a two-story house, Berg's buildings are houses of cards—literally. Bryan has captured the Guinness World Record at least ten times since 1992 for building the world's tallest house of cards. His most recent Guinness record was a 25-foot-tall, 2,400-deck, 133-card-level-high house he made in Berlin. It weighed about 200 pounds and took Berg two weeks to complete. He never glues, tapes, bends, notches, or folds, and he never goes over budget, since his only building material is cards—and cheap ones at that. Berg claims that when it comes to building houses, the lower the quality cards the better. (He's sounding more and more like a builder I know.) "Shitty cards are key," he says.

A 1997 graduate of Iowa State's architecture program and currently a special lecturer at Iowa State's College of Design, Berg began stacking the decks at the tender age of eight after watching his grandfather stack cards for fun. And Berg kept on stacking them, buying whole cases of cards at a time from his hometown Hy-Vee in Spirit Lake and moving ever closer to the ceiling of the family's home. At the age of seventeen, before he had even earned his high school diploma, he broke his first Guinness World Record for freestanding card structures with a 14-foot tower. And it's more than likely that Berg is the only student in Iowa State history to completely fund his education by building with cards.

Now that Berg has made the big time, he has an agent, Omaha-based Dean Short, whose Dean Short Talent Service specializes in fair and festival acts such as Steve Trash, "who makes magic out of trash for educational fun," and Cousin Grumpy's Pork Chop Show (don't ask). Over the years at fairs, conventions, and festivals around the world, Berg has made almost every structure imaginable, from pyramids to classic ballparks (including Philadelphia's Veterans Stadium and Brooklyn's Ebbetts Field) to the Empire State Building. Berg was even featured on *Ripley's Believe It or Not* for his scale replica of the Iowa State Capitol at the 2000 Iowa State Fair.

So how does he do it? With gravity and patience, he'll quip. But if you really want to build like Berg, you're going to have to buy his 2003 book, *Stacking the Deck: Secrets of the World's Master Card Architect.* Coauthored by Berg and Thomas O'Donnell, former *Des Moines Register* reporter, the book gives you step-by-step instructions and lots of helpful illustrations for building your own card creations. So what to do when you accidentally knock down a towering card house, as you're sure to do many times? The master recommends staying calm, and he's learned how to do so himself the hard way—lots of experience. You might also consider stealing another page from Berg's book by breaking out the leaf blower to help clean up the mess.

None of Berg's work is on permanent display because it's liable to blow over. You can reach his agent, Dean Short, at (402) 553–3502.

EVER MEET A WIND FARMER?
Storm Lake

One of the world's biggest farms is located right here in northwest Iowa, but it doesn't produce a single pound of pork, gallon of milk, or bushel of corn or soy. And it's harvest time year-round on this farm, twenty-four hours a day, seven days a week. (Sounds like a farmer's worst nightmare.)

Dedicated in 1999, the Storm Lake wind-power facility is the largest wind-generated power facility in the world. With 262 wind turbines spread over hundreds of acres between Cherokee and Buena Vista Counties, the facility generates 650,000 megawatt-hours of clean electricity, enough to fulfill the energy needs of about 64,000 average Midwestern homes, that is, those without three or more teenagers living inside. Each wind turbine is composed of a tower (vaguely resembling a high-tension electrical tower) topped with three 79-foot blades. Weighing in excess of 5,300 pounds each, these blades are aerodynamically designed to produce lift much as an airplane wing does, so they only require an 8-mile-per-hour wind to turn them.

If you drive west on Highway 7 out of Storm Lake, the wind turbines are visible to the north. The farmers make money by leasing the turbine land to the power company, the state gets some pollution-free energy, and drivers get something new to look at as they're cruising the back roads of Iowa. There's something slightly surreal about the rows and rows of turbines looming giantlike above the farmhouses and fields of corn, their 200-foot-high rotors spinning slowly in the wind. But the strangeness is all for a good cause: The wind farm helps keep thousands off tons of carbon dioxide and sulfur emissions out of our air (and lungs).

A windmill arm for the twenty-first century.

At the corner of Highway Street and East Lake Shore Drive in Storm Lake, you can find a single turbine blade from one of the towers (either that or it's a very long canoe). A present to Storm Lake from Enron, the power company that built the wind farm, the blade makes for a pretty striking town sculpture.

The turbine blade is located at the corner of Highway Street and East Lake Shore Drive, just east of downtown. Located in both Buena Vista and Cherokee Counties, the wind farm is visible from Highway 7 west of Storm Lake.

A MUSEUM THAT KEEPS GROWING
Storm Lake

The Living Heritage Tree Museum, located in Sunset Park on the shores of Storm Lake, is an outdoor museum planted with fifty-one trees grown from seedlings and cuttings of trees associated with more or less famous people and events. One of my favorites is the Moon Tree, an American sycamore grown from a seed that was brought to the moon and back by crewmen of the Apollo 12 flight. Come to think of it, the park is heavy on flight-associated people and events: There's a crabapple obtained from the home of Charles Lindbergh, who made the first solo flight across the Atlantic in 1927, a butternut from the Hamlin, West Virginia home of Chuck Yeager, who on October 14, 1947, became the first man to fly faster than the speed of sound, and a walnut descended from a tree that Orville and Wilbur Wright planted at their airfield outside of Dayton, Ohio.

One of the pleasures of the Living Heritage Tree Museum is wondering about the personality (or personalities) behind the tree selections. Stan Lemaster and Theodore Klein made the park possible by donating the heritage trees to Storm Lake. Lemaster, a retired General Electric computer engineer from Louisville, Kentucky, came up with the idea for heritage trees during a bout of insomnia. Some of their selections are no-brainers, trees that anyone would want to have in their Living Heritage Tree Collection; a George Washington tulip poplar, an Abraham Lincoln white oak, a Ulysses S. Grant gum tree. But then there are a few surprises. How about the Ann Rutledge maple, grown from a maple shading the grave of Abraham Lincoln's alleged first sweetheart, whose death, according to the little plaque in front of the tree, was BELIEVED TO BE RESPONSIBLE

FOR HIS MELANCHOLY DISPOSITION. Then there's the Colonel Harlan Sanders ash, from the home of Colonel Sanders in Shelbyville, Kentucky—yup, the same Colonel Sanders who became world-famous for his secret-recipe fried chicken. We can easily forgive Lemaster for playing local favorites, though.

The park also features some descendants of trees famous in their own right, including a delicious-apple tree, which originally grew by chance in Peru, Iowa, and was chopped down twice before owners figured out they had a good thing growing. Then there's an offspring of the Sir Isaac Newton apple tree, the famous tree that dropped a gravitational discovery right onto Newton's head. None of the trees are quite mature yet, though, so if you're looking to be struck with your own apple of insight, you're going to have to wait a while.

The Living Heritage Tree Museum is located in Sunset Park on West Lake Shore Drive, right on Storm Lake. Take West Fifth Street to Ontario Street, head south toward the lake, and the museum will be right in front of you. For information call (712) 732–3780.

O NE OF THE M ANY E IGHTH W ONDERS OF THE W ORLD
West Bend

The glossy tourist brochure for West Bend's Grotto of the Redemption makes the rather dubious but hard-to-refute claim that the structure is "frequently considered the Eighth Wonder of the World." Though it may or may not be among the world's top eight, or even top ten, wonders, the grotto definitely tops the list of Iowa wonders.

As large as a city block, more than 40 feet tall at its highest point, and composed of the largest collection of minerals and semiprecious stones in the world, the Grotto of the Redemption is both a shrine honoring the life of Jesus Christ and a monument to one man's obsession with rocks, minerals, and geodes. Father Paul Dobberstein began construction on the grotto as a young priest in 1912 and worked continuously on the project over the next four decades until his death in 1954. In summertime he worked outdoors, building the grotto by hand, stone by stone, without the aid of machinery, save for an electric hoist that he purchased in 1947. During the long winter months, he built sections of the grotto indoors, carefully setting beautiful stones, minerals, shells, and corals into large sections of concrete. In spring and fall Father Dobberstein traveled the country and the world in search of building materials for his ever-expanding shrine: agates from Brazil, Mexico, and Madagascar, azurite and malachite from the Ural Mountains of Russia, stalactites and stalagmites from caves in South Dakota and the Ozarks, pipe-organ coral from Hawaii, amethysts from the Andes, to name just a sampling. All told, Dobberstein traveled more than 800,000 miles in his hunt for unique rocks and minerals, and experts now assess the geologic value of the grotto at more than $4 million. When, or if, he ever had time to give a sermon, marry a couple, or baptize a child, we haven't been able to ascertain.

The Grotto of the Redemption is, technically speaking, a conglomeration of nine separate grottos, or cavernlike structures, each one highlighting an important event in the life of Jesus, from his birth to his resurrection. Taking it all in is dizzying, to say the least. In addition to the concrete, rocks, and minerals, the grotto also contains colored glass, tile, shells of every shape and size, and petrified wood, all arranged in intricate patterns to create the structure's many caves, arches, hollows, and stairways. The end result is a paradoxical ordered chaos. The grotto seems as much a work of nature as it does a man-made structure, with a roof that resembles mountain peaks shaped by wind and water instead of a builder's hand.

The grotto is flanked by the Grotto Park Restaurant, the Grotto Gift Shop, the Grotto Museum, and a beautiful Spanish

Can you call four decades of grotto building a hobby?
Photo: Catherine Cole

Mission–style Catholic church (where Dobberstein would have presumably led his congregation in prayer if he hadn't been hunting for azurite and malachite from the Ural Mountains), complete with bell tower and red-tile roof. The museum contains a large display of some of the precious and semiprecious stones used in the construction of the grotto, as well as some early newspaper articles about Father Dobberstein and the shrine.

The Grotto of the Redemption is located in West Bend. Just follow the signs on Highway 15 as you enter town. For more information or for group reservations, call (515) 887–2371 or (800) 868–3641.

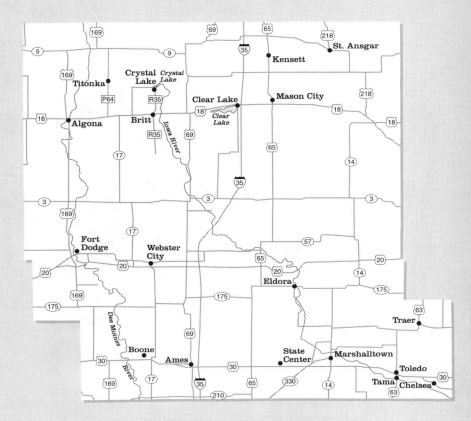

NORTH CENTRAL

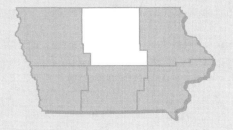

NORTH CENTRAL

A CHEESY ATTRACTION
Algona

In March of 2003 a man in Hawaii poured a single-serving bag of Cheetos into a bowl and out tumbled an unusually large morsel of cheesy, fried snack food that would forever change the history of one small Iowa town.

The man did what any red-blooded, technologically savvy American capitalist would do: He auctioned the Cheeto off on eBay, billing it as the world's largest. (Original reports called it "the size of a small lemon," though in actuality it's about as big as a chicken nugget.) His prospective sale caught the eyes of Internet-surfing folks across the country, including Bryce Wilson, a deejay in Algona looking for something to talk about on the air. Bryce started a pledge drive to bring the Cheeto to town as a tourist attraction. "I got on the air that day and said, 'This is our chance! We're going to get ourselves on the map today! People will come from miles around! We'll need new roads just to accommodate all the traffic! It will be great for the economy!'" Bryce said. He raised $180.

In the meantime online bidding for the Cheeto twice reached $99 million before eBay yanked it. Of course, no one had intentions of paying such a price, so the Cheeto's owner turned to his one serious offer, the community of Algona. He donated the Cheeto to the city, requesting that the $180 go to a local charity in his name.

*Iowa's most famous piece
of overpuffed snack food.*
Photo: Clint Buckner

News of the Cheeto's sale spread across the country, and the
story was reported on Web sites, in newspapers and on radio
stations around the world, including CNN and a radio station
in Australia. General Electric custom-made a bulletproof glass
case for it. A New York glassblower blew a swirly orange
pedestal for it. Locally, there was some controversy over the
misshapen piece of snack food. Some thought the media stir
ridiculous; others thought it just plain fun; some even threatened to kidnap the Cheeto: C.L.A.M, the Cheeto Liberation
Army of Men, as well as the women's organization, C.L.A.W.,
and one lone man calling himself Crouching Cheeto, Hidden
HoHo.

In the end, though, the Cheeto made it safely to its unveiling at Sister Sarah's Bar & Restaurant (thanks, in part, to a police and fire-truck escort). The national late-night TV talk show *Jimmy Kimmel LIVE* broadcast the event via satellite. Residents packed the place, wearing Cheeto T-shirts, hats, and jewelry. The mayor even gave a speech, declaring March 13 Giant Cheeto Day in Algona.

After the unveiling much of the fervor died down. People still visit Sarah's specifically to see the Cheeto, which sits on a velvet pillow on its custom-blown stand in its custom-made case on the mantel. There are no T-shirts for sale, no signs outside of Sarah's, not even a billboard anywhere in town. Its presence is requested in area parades and at local high schools, but for the most part, it's back to business as usual in Algona. Bryce thinks it might be a few years before residents are willing to embrace their new attraction wholeheartedly.

"Some people are kind of sick of it now, for obvious reasons," he says. "But I'm quite happy to spread the joy of the Cheeto."

The World's Largest Cheeto is on display at Sister Sarah's Bar & Restaurant in Algona. Take U.S. Highway 18 west off I–35 in Clear Lake, and Sarah's is on the south side of the highway as you head into town. Call (712) 295–7757 for more information.

GERMAN POWS BUILD CHRISTMAS SCENE — DRAW CROWDS
Algona

One of Algona's star attractions, a sixty-piece, half-life-sized nativity scene, can be visited only during the Christmas holiday season. This was a specific request made by German prisoner of war Eduard Kaib, who built the scene because he missed his family while he was at a base camp near Algona in 1944.

During the Second World War, there were prison camps in most states, and this one—with an average of 3,000 prisoners, nearly the population of Algona at the time—processed German POWs for thirty-four branch camps in Minnesota, Iowa, and the Dakotas. Were they located here, smack-dab in the middle of the country, because the absence of an ocean lent no hope of escape? Because Iowa men fighting overseas had farmland that needed attention and prisoners were cheap labor? Because Vice President-at-the-time Henry Wallace was an Iowan concerned with the economic and labor needs of his home state? No one seems to know for sure, but it's estimated that this particular camp system's prisoners completed about $3.5 million worth of work.

The prisoners were treated well. They had an orchestra, a chorus, and a dramatic club. They had canteen accounts that were credited 80 cents a day for their labor, with which they bought things like magazine subscriptions and sports equipment. Eduard Kaib, an architect and noncommissioned officer of the German army, bought building materials.

He especially missed his home and family during the Christmas holidays and so set about building a nativity scene as a way to cure his loneliness. Five other POWs helped him. Over the course of a year, they hand-carved plaster set upon heavy concrete-covered wood-and-wire frames for all sixty pieces of the scene, from the baby Jesus and the Wise Men to sheep and camels. The scene was completed in 1945, and when the camp was disbanded in 1946, Eduard left the scene in Algona, with three requests: that it stay in Algona, that there never be an admission charge to view it, and that it be viewed only at Christmastime.

His requests have been honored. Each December, thousands of people visit the scene in its own climate-controlled building at the local fairgrounds. Visitors have come from all fifty states and around the world. Eduard (now deceased) even returned once, and Algona residents gave him a grand reception. He came during the Christmas holiday season of 1968, and he brought his family.

Algona's nativity scene can be viewed for free in December at the Kossuth County Fairground, located south of Algona at US 169 and Fair Street. Open daily from 2:00 to 9:00 P.M. and on Sundays and Christmas Day from noon to 9:00 P.M. Special showings and tour groups on request. For more information call the First United Methodist Men's Club at (515) 295–7241 or the Algona Area Chamber of Commerce at (515) 295–7201 or visit www.pwcamp.algona.org.

S O T H A T ' S W H A T A C O W S P E C U L U M L O O K S L I K E
A m e s

At Iowa State's museum of veterinary history, located in the R. Allen Packer Veterinary Heritage Room, the only things more scary than the equine dental tools and bovine reproductive instruments (circa 1930), are the mostly unlabeled photographs of diseased and deceased animals.

The R. Allen Packer Veterinary Heritage Room, a curious collection of old texts, instruments, medicines, audiovisual materials, and, as we mentioned, photographs, all related to the study and "care" of animals. (It's a little hard to associate the word care with a pair of 2-foot-long iron Cattle Nose Tongs, or a stainless-steel Hog Ear Notcher.) The museum is dedicated to the memory of Dr. R. Allen Packer, an Iowa State professor in Veterinary Medicine from 1940 to 1985, whose credentials include serving as head of the Department of Veterinary Microbiology and Preventive Medicine for almost thirty years, coauthoring three major veterinary texts, and, as an Iowa State undergrad, participating on the meat-judging team.

In addition to historical information on the leading role played by Ames veterinarians in conquering everything from bovine TB to hog cholera, the collection contains more than 1,500 historic books and journals, a number of eighteenth- and nineteenth-century microscopes, and a minipharmacy with medicines from the preantibiotic 1920s, including a small but potent can of DDT for fleas (poor old toxic Rover), canine diarrhea tablets (ingredients not listed), and mercury, used, of course, as an antacid. But the shocking highlights of the collection (for us anyway), are the very large, very frightening dental and surgical instruments, like the 3-foot-long forceps, the stainless-steel calf puller, and the gouges, chisels, and molar punches, all of which look more like mining tools than medical instruments.

Rest assured, though, animal health care wasn't all heavy artillery back in the old days. Veterinarians also seemed to be interested in alternative, or what we now like to call complementary, medicine: The museum contains a set of nineteenth-century animal acupuncture needles, used, presumably, to manage lower back pain in mules and help hogs give up cigarettes.

The R. Allen Packer Veterinary Heritage Room is located just off the library in Iowa State's College of Veterinary Medicine. From Elwood Drive take a right onto South Sixteenth Street and follow to the College of Veterinary Medicine. During the academic year the museum is open Monday through Thursday, 8:00 A.M. to 10:00 P.M.; Friday, 8:00 A.M. to 5:00 P.M.; Saturday, 9:00 A.M. to 5:00 P.M.; and Sunday, 2:00 to 10:00 P.M.

KATE SHELLEY'S MIDNIGHT HEROICS
Boone

The story of Kate Shelley's heroics sounds like something straight out of Hollywood: late evening, torrential rains and a violent thunderstorm, a washed-out railroad bridge, and Kate Shelley, the seventeen-year-old heroine, crawling on her hands and knees across a 671-foot-long railroad bridge to save the midnight express and its 200 passengers from a tragic fate. Quite fittingly, she was rewarded with everything from a free lifetime pass on the railroad to the honor of having a very impressive bridge named after her, the Kate Shelley High Bridge, located just west of Boone, the longest and highest double-track railroad bridge in the world.

The more detailed story goes like this: Kate Shelley, her mother, and her four younger siblings (Kate's father died when she was only fourteen) lived in a small house on the banks of Honey Creek, right beside the railroad bridge. On July 6, 1881, a fierce rainstorm caused flooding, which threatened the Shelley's barn and home, and so before nightfall, Kate moved the livestock to higher ground to protect them from the rising waters. The storm raged on into the night, and Kate and her mom stayed up to keep watch on the swollen creek as the younger children slept. Some time before midnight they heard a tremendous crunching sound as the bridge over Honey Creek, weakened by the floodwaters, gave way beneath a pusher engine with a crew of four, sent from Moingona to test the tracks as far as Boone.

Kate knew the Chicago-bound midnight express, due to pass from the west over first the Des Moines River Bridge and then the now washed-out Honey Creek Bridge, had to be stopped. In the thunder and lightning and torrential rain, she set out with a lantern for Moingona to alert the stationmaster.

A little girl who deserved to have a big bridge named after her.

Though the station house was only a mile away, in between was the 50-foot-high Des Moines River Bridge, the raging floodwaters just yards below the tracks. Its cross ties were laid almost 3 feet apart to discourage people from walking across it, so Kate crawled. From timber to timber, an extinguished lantern clutched tightly in her hand, the flood-swollen waters of the Des Moines roaring below her, the powerful storm winds threatening to topple her from the bridge, Kate crawled the 671 perilous feet on her hands and knees. When she finally made it to the Moingona station, she was so exhausted that her speech was nearly incomprehensible. The men at the station reportedly thought she had gone crazy, but then they understood: "Stop the express, the Honey Creek Bridge is down!"

After the deed Kate weathered a media onslaught and didn't get out of bed for thirty days. She received gifts of money and goods from passengers, from the State of Iowa ($200), from the Chicago-Northwestern Railroad ($100, a half barrel of flour, half a load of coal, a gold watch and a lifetime pass), and was offered free tuition at Simpson College in Indianola, where she planned to study to become a teacher. In 1903, after teaching for a number of years in Boone County, Kate was offered the job of stationmaster at Moingona, the very site of her heroics, and she served there until 1910, receiving so many visitors requesting her autograph and photo that she had hundreds of postcards of herself made up, which she sold, according to one report, "at a very small profit."

Located a few miles west of Boone and just a stone's throw away from the now-abandoned bridge Kate crossed that fateful night back in 1881, the Kate Shelley High Bridge, a steel-beam structure 186 feet high and stretching over a half mile between bluffs along the Des Moines river, looks far more Western than Midwestern. (Gazing at that half mile of crisscrossing I-beams from below, I kept expecting to see the Rockies looming on the horizon.) Completed in 1901, the bridge has been in operation for more than one hundred years and still sees quite a bit of traffic, an average of fifty trains a day. The Boone and Scenic Valley Railroad even offers a daily 12-mile trip in vintage

1920s rail cars, offering a breathtaking view of the bridge and the Des Moines River valley.

The old railway station at Moingona where Kate worked is now the site of the Kate Shelley Railroad Museum and Park. You can learn more about Kate's life there—not an easy one, in spite of the generosity of those so impressed by her bravery—and you can even buy postcards of the heroine, sold at a very small profit, of course. Kate Shelley would have approved.

For more information about the Kate Shelley Railroad Museum, located at 1198 232nd Street in Moingona, call (515) 432–1907. The Kate Shelley High Bridge is located 3 miles west of Boone on J Avenue. Follow Eighth Street west to the T intersection with Marion Avenue. Take a right onto Marion, cross the railroad tracks, and then take a left onto 198th Road. Follow the signs to the Kate Shelley High Bridge. And for more information about the Boone & Scenic Valley Railroad, located at 225 Tenth Street in Boone, call (800) 626–0319. The railroad offers weekday train rides over the bridge at 1:30 P.M. and twice-daily weekend and holiday rides at 1:30 and 4:00 P.M.

CONVENTION DRESS CODE: RAILROAD CASUAL
Britt

A quick run through the National Hobo Convention in Britt could leave you wondering why present-day hobos look eerily like residents of a small Iowa town. But Britt's hobos are actually residents of this small Iowa town; after all, the convention is their celebration.

And the hobos are there (look for characteristic railroad touches such as overalls, train-conductor hats, bandanas, and backpacks). They're just heavily outnumbered by the residents,

Can someone tell me where to find the panel discussion on advances in campfire cooking?
Photo: Clint Buckner

which makes sense considering that the number of hobos nationwide has dwindled to a few hundred (down from a few hundred thousand during the hobo heyday of the Great Depression). But these wandering railriders still do exist, believe it or not, and though there are hobo conventions throughout the country, this one, started in 1900, is the grand-daddy of them all. The town is also home to a hobo foundation, the country's only hobo museum, and the world's only hobo memorial.

Hobos and residents alike gather here annually during the second weekend in August for rickety carnival rides, a flea market, museum tours, free mulligan stew, and the crowning of the king and queen of the hobos. Hobo Spike and Mama Jo won the 2003 election, which was held under the city park pavilion and decided, as usual, by applause. The two will spend the next year traveling the country (a given, really, considering they're hobos) promoting Britt and the national convention.

After the election Hobo Spike caught his breath behind the counter at the Hobo Museum, when a woman with her son, who had never seen a real live hobo before, spied his bandana. "You're a hobo, aren't you?" she asked. The answer came, better than she could have dreamed: "I'm the king of the hobos," he said proudly. The wide-eyed boy went back to meet the king, and the mingling of hobos and nonhobos at this historic hobo gathering continued.

The National Hobo Convention takes place the second week in August in Britt, located west of Clear Lake on US 18. For more information contact the Britt Chamber of Commerce at (641) 843–3867 or visit www.brittchamberofcommerce.com.

SMART, TALENTED, BUT VERY LOUD WHEN WORKING
Chelsea

Most of us don't think about coon dogs often enough to wonder where the capital of coon doggery might be. Well, now we know: it's Coon Dog Acres, in between Tama and Chelsea on County Road E64.

Terry Daniels, a retiree who worked at Fisher Instruments in Marshalltown for many years, built dog heaven in a quiet valley just off a twisting county highway. He's been breeding

*Good coon dogs don't necessarily make
good neighbors.*

beagles and coon dogs since 1966, but now he's more interested
in training dogs than selling them. If you visit and convince
him of the sincerity of your interest in the sport, though, you
might just walk away with a talented canine pup at a good
price. And your new pooch is likely to have a pretty impressive
pedigree, too—Old Duke, the current world champion coon
dog, is a fifth-generation offspring of the first dogs Terry
raised back in the sixties.

Terry Daniel's place is at 2120 County Road E64, a road
that runs between Chelsea and Tama. Terry comes and goes, so
you'll want to call ahead first. (641) 484-3994.

GROOVIN' AT THE SURF
Clear Lake

The Surf Ballroom is famous for being the venue where Buddy Holly, Ritchie Valens, and Jiles P. "the Big Bopper" Richardson played their last show before dying in a plane crash in a farmer's field 5 miles north of town. For visitors primarily interested in the so-called Day the Music Died, there's a stone monument to the trio just outside the Surf as well as a memorial inside that fills quite a few feet of wall space, including large photographs of Valens, Holly, and Richardson, posters advertising the fateful Winter Dance Party on February 2, 1959, newspaper articles, and more.

But if you venture past the memorial, you'll find there's quite a bit more to the Surf than the story of the events of that tragic night. For starters the Surf is a true rarity, an authentic ballroom from the heyday of the Big Bands that looks as if it's passed through the years unchanged. High vaulted ceilings, beautiful hardwood floors, booths against the walls of the main dance hall, tables beside the dance floor, all the night-club details feel so familiar (either from your past if you're a certain age or from movies if you're a lot younger than a certain age) that stepping out onto the Surf's 6,300-square-foot dance floor feels like a strange sort of homecoming. If you want to take a more detailed trip down memory lane, the Surf's Hall of Fame contains photos, autographs, and other memorabilia from the Big Band era. And be sure to check the wall backstage for the signatures of past performers at the Surf.

Though the Surf is located just across the street from Clear Lake, there really isn't any surf to speak of, across the road or even within 1,000 miles of the club's doors. But in the service of good old-fashioned escapism, the Surf was fashioned to

The way rock 'n' roll used to be.

resemble a South Seas beach club, with puffy white clouds on the ceiling and oceanfront murals behind the main stage and along the walls, featuring long stretches of sandy beach, palm trees, sailboats, and, of course, some foamy surf. Did someone say piña colada?

The Surf, located at 460 North Shore Drive, is open to the public from 9:00 A.M. to 5:00 P.M. daily and plays host to a variety of rock 'n' roll, jazz, blues, and Big Band acts throughout the year. For more information or a schedule of events, call (641) 357–6151.

THE FIELD WHERE THE MUSIC DIED

*I*n the early morning of February 3, 1959, the plane carrying Buddy Holly, Ritchie Valens, Jiles P. "the Big Bopper"
Richardson, and pilot Roger Peterson, crashed in a farmer's
field 5 miles north of Clear Lake and came to rest along a
fencerow. Even though the exact spot went unmarked for
many years, fans of the trio still walked into the cornfields
to pay their respects and leave flowers and other mementos.
But according to Ken Paquette, a fan from Portersfield, Wisconsin, because there was no memorial, people didn't know
exactly where to pay their respects and where to leave their
offerings. "People really weren't sure where it was," he said,
"and I thought there should be something there."

So in honor of the three musicians he built a small stainless-steel monument composed of a guitar engraved with
their names along with three stainless-steel 45s, each one
engraved with the title of one of their hit songs: Holly's
"Peggy Sue," Valens's "Donna," and the Big Bopper's "Chan-
tilly Lace." And now that people know where to leave their
"gifts," there's no shortage of odd stuff at the site. Surrounding the monument when we visited were faded plastic flowers,
lightly coated with dust; some coins (mostly pennies) scattered on the ground; six lighters; twelve pens; a faded Cubs
cap; too many business cards to count, including one from a
policeman in Fort Madison and one from a tire salesman in
Sioux City; a health-insurance card from Connecticut; an
American Airlines Advantage card; a couple of wallet-sized
family portraits; seven or eight large, cloth-covered elastic
ponytail holders; and a card from a local corn maze with a
start time of 5:05 P.M. and a finish time of 5:31 P.M.

Holly arranged for the private flight out of Mason City
Airport after enduring a brutally cold trip across Iowa on a
tour bus that had developed heating-system problems; it was
reported that one drummer even got frostbite. He and his

The field where the music died.

CONTINUED

two backup musicians, Waylon Jennings (yup, the same Waylon Jennings who's now a country-and-western sensation) and Tommy Allsup, would travel to the next show in comfort, and with the time they gained on the rest of the musicians, the group planned to do their laundry (even stars have to wash their socks). After hearing that the Big Bopper was running a fever, presumably from the bus ride from hell, Jennings graciously gave up his seat on the flight. When Holly heard Jennings wasn't going to fly, he said to him, "Well, I hope your old bus freezes up." Without missing a beat Waylon Jennings replied, "Well, I hope your plane crashes." (Jennings reportedly relived that brief exchange for years.) Tommy Allsup offered to flip Ritchie Valens for the remaining seat and, in losing the coin toss, saved his own life.

Investigators never determined the precise cause of the crash, though they speculated that inclement weather—a light dusting of snow fell that night—and pilot error were contributing factors. The deaths of three hit musicians prompted newspapers to call the tragedy "The Day the Music Died," and Don McLean later memorialized the trio, and the phrase, in his hit "American Pie." The plaintive melancholy of that song perfectly matches the loneliness and isolation of the spot where the plane that carried Holly, Valens, and Richardson came to rest, beside a fence in a field of corn miles outside of town.

From US 18 in Clear Lake, go north on North Eighth Street for 4.7 miles. When the road starts to curve left, take a right onto 310th Street, a gravel road, and then take the first left onto Gull Avenue. Follow Gull Avenue north for about .5 mile, just past the grain bins to the first fencerow. There's space to park on the right side of the road. Walk west along the fencerow for about a half mile until you reach the memorial.

PYRAMID FOR RENT
Clear Lake

If you happen to be in the market for a short-term pyramid rental in north-central Iowa but just haven't found what you're looking for, then look no more. The Pyramid House, located just across the street from 3,600-acre Clear Lake, one of the largest spring-fed lakes in Iowa, is available for both weekly and monthly rentals. Though the Pyramid House is definitely on the smallish side for a pyramid—with 5,500 square

A little bit of Egypt in Iowa.

feet of space and a height of only about 37 feet, it's downright puny compared to the 482-foot-high, thirteen-acre Great Pyramid in Egypt—it's a pretty spacious lake rental. And with five bedrooms, three bathrooms, and a two-and-a-half-car garage, you can bring your kids, your friends, and your friends' kids, as well as that half car you rarely get to drive, and make a week of it.

One of the house's strong points (besides the actual one on top), are the many large windows looking south onto the lake; almost every room fills with sunlight and offers a beautiful view. Other features include two decks, Italian marble floors, and a long dock across the street for sunbathing and swimming. And if you tire of the sun and water or if the rain comes, the Surf Ballroom, Clear Lake's famous musical venue, is just a few blocks down the street. Don't even bother checking the basement for sarcophagi, though. Either there never were any, or they were in violation of code and the rental inspectors made the owners haul them away.

The Pyramid House is located at 1102 North Shore Drive. Both weekly and monthly rentals are available. For rates and more information, call Jody Eastman at (515) 771–3647 or (515) 277–3647.

A BIG ONE THAT CAN'T GET AWAY
Crystal Lake

Weighing in at around 1,650 pounds and with a total nose-to-tail-tip length of some 17 feet 8 inches, Crystal Lake's famed bullhead is a fish that even the most unscrupulous teller of fish tales could be honest about. "He must have weighed almost two tons," he could say, without batting an eye. "As big as Shamu at Sea World and a whole lot uglier, too. Could have swallowed me and Ed whole and still had room left over to down the cooler of beer for dessert." And every word of it would be true.

The statue, hailed as the World's Largest Bullhead, was built in 1958, and ever since then it's served as a town mascot, prime snapshot spot, and mighty tough yardstick (or five and a half yardsticks, to be more exact) by which locals might measure their own angling achievements.

The World's Largest Bullhead is located at the end of Main Street on the shore of 263-acre Crystal Lake.

A MOVIE SITE, B&B, RV PARK, AND FIGURE-EIGHT DIRT RACETRACK IN ONE
Eldora

C huck Welch, owner of the farmhouse devastated in the climactic scene of the 1996 movie *Twister,* is nothing if not enterprising. When I visited, he was sitting on his back steps, dressed in a cap, a polo shirt, and faded blue jeans, having a beer with the man who had just carved a figure-eight dirt racetrack in the cornfields just east of the house. "I've got the house, the RV park, a bed-and-breakfast, and now I'm going to have racing out here," he told me, with a hint of pride in his voice. Since his prices are so reasonable, perhaps he's wise to diversify. Chuck charges $2.00 for a tour, $7.95 for an RV site, and an astonishingly low $19.95 for a one-night stay in the 1891 Sears-catalog house B&B. (The cook got sick and wasn't able to come back to work, so now Chuck runs the B&B but offers only one of the Bs.)

Twister, a movie about two groups of rival scientists in Oklahoma racing to be the first to launch packs of sensors into a tornado, features a thin plot, lots of storm chasing, some

A house that's been through Hollywood hell and back and lived to sell the tale.

mesmerizing special effects, and a bang-up climactic tornado scene—filmed, of course, at Chuck's farmhouse—in which tools go crazy, a fence explodes, and film scientists Jo and Bill Harding (Helen Hunt and Bill Paxton) tie themselves to a pipe in the pump house to avoid being blown away. Warner Brothers spent sixty days getting the farmhouse—which had stood vacant for twenty-seven years—ready for filming at a cost of $50,000 a day. They repaired and built outbuildings and fences, planted a whole slew of sunflowers along the driveway (and delayed filming twice to make sure the flowers were in peak bloom), and spruced up the house with new shingles and five coats of paint. After preparations were complete and the sunflowers looked radiant, the 250-plus-person crew spent thirteen days filming at the site at a cost of about $1,000,000 a day. Along the way the crew destroyed outbuildings, fences, and flowers and sand-blasted the house and its five coats of fresh paint to give it that just-been-to-hell-and-back look that's oh-so-popular with home owners.

Now the house looks to be on the mend, but it still could use a little TLC. Chuck uses the proceeds from his many enter-prises, including the gift shop in the parlor where he sells T-shirts, hats, and photographs of the house (at $5 apiece or 3 for $10), to pay for ongoing improvements and renovations, like the figure-eight track out back. "The place is all mine," he said. "I bought it with a lawyer in town just before Warner Brothers came in, but he sold me his share, and now I have the house and all the headaches, too. But it's all paid off." And if the racetrack can draw a crowd, and people start buying more three-packs of Twister House photos, then maybe Chuck can make a little money, too.

The Twister House is located 3 miles east of Eldora at 26302 Y Avenue. Take Highway 175 east out of Eldora about 3 miles, and then take a right on Y Avenue. The Twister House will be a mile or two south on the east side of the road. For more infor-mation call Chuck Welch at (515) 858–5133.

A GENUINE REPRODUCTION OF A FAMOUS FAKE
Fort Dodge

Fort Dodge is the original home of the Cardiff Giant, a 10-foot-tall statue with 21-inch feet that has been called "the greatest hoax in history." We say his original home because Old Hoaxey, as nineteenth-century fans started calling him, was sculpted from a massive five-ton block of Fort Dodge gypsum. And even though the original Cardiff Giant resides at the Farmer's Museum in Cooperstown, New York, Fort Dodge is still home to the Cardiff Giant, or one of the Cardiff giants. (There are four that we know about, but there could be many, many more.) You can visit him, or a re-creation of him, at the Fort Museum, a re-creation (sense a pattern here?) of the fort built in 1862 to protect local residents from Indian raids.

The story of the Cardiff Giant is as intriguing as a soap opera love affair. George Hull, an atheist cigarmaker from Binghamton, New York, reportedly came up with the idea after arguing with a revivalist minister about the absurdity of a biblical passage referring to antediluvian giants: "There were giants in the earth in those days" (Genesis 6:4). Hull traveled to Fort Dodge, ordered a five-ton gypsum block to go (claiming he needed the stone for patriotic statuary), oversaw the sculpting and aging process in Chicago of a giant, supine man, hips canted, right arm draped across his chest, and then buried the statue at his brother-in-law William "Stub" Newell's farm in Cardiff, New York, a region already known for its fossils.

About a year later on Saturday, October 16, 1869, Stub Newell hired workmen to dig a well in the exact spot where he and Hull had buried the giant; about 3 feet down, they struck one of his huge feet and then quickly set about uncovering all ten feet. Word of the "discovery" quickly spread, and soon hundreds of people were visiting Newell's farm every day, paying 50-cents apiece for a look at what some speculated was the petrified body of a member of the ancient race of giants mentioned in Genesis. On October 23, Stub Newell, acting on Hull's behalf, sold a three-fourths interest in the giant to five local businessmen for $30,000, a very healthy return on Hull's $2,600 investment. In order to accommodate larger crowds, the group moved the giant to Syracuse, where press attention and speculation about his origins intensified. One expert, Dr. John F.

Boynton, rejected the antediluvian giant theory and hypothe-
sized that it was a statue created by a seventeenth-century
Jesuit missionary to awe local Indian tribes. Still, the crowds of
giant-lovers kept coming.

By November, though, the hoax started to unravel. Farmers
in the area reported having seen a very large crate being
unloaded at the Newell farm, and a Yale paleontologist, Othniel
C. March, citing fresh chisel marks, pronounced the giant a
"decided humbug of recent origin." On December 10 Hull came
clean, but at that point, it didn't seem to matter. The crowds
were still coming, and still paying, to see the fake from Fort
Dodge. P. T. Barnum even offered $60,000 to rent the giant for
a three-month circus stint, but the group had already decided
to take him on the road themselves and refused. Barnum commissioned a fake of the fake, made of wood and covered in plaster, and when the original fake and the facsimile of the fake
were displayed that December in New York City just 2 blocks
apart, the Barnum fake reportedly outdrew the original. Tough
crowd.

Just in case you want to make a road trip, you can visit the
original Barnum fake at Marvin's Marvelous Mechanical
Museum in Farmington Hills, Michigan; or, if you're interested
in seeing a fake of Barnum's fake of Hull's fake, you can visit
Circus World in Baraboo, Wisconsin; but here in Fort Dodge,
you can visit a fake of the original phony, made from the very
same Fort Dodge gypsum. Think of him as the Cardiff giant's
honest brother, a giant who never pretended to be anything
other than what he was: a big fake.

The Fort Museum, which contains a complete frontier village as well as the Cardiff Giant replica, is located a quarter
mile east of the intersection of U.S. Highways 169 and 20. It's
open May through October, from 9:00 A.M. to 6:00 P.M. daily.
For more information call (515) 573–4231.

LONG BEARD GOES TO WASHINGTON
Kensett

When Russell Langseth found his late grandfather's beard in an attic chest in 1967, he did what any respectful, legacy-minded descendant would have done: He packed the beard up and shipped it to the Smithsonian Institution in Washington D.C. Of course, it wasn't just any old beard. After receiving the facial hair, a Mrs. Lucille St. Hayne of the Smithsonian replied, "So far as we have been able to determine, the beard not only is an artifact, but an all-time record. One can only admire the grower's tenacity, to say nothing of the ability to avoid stepping on it." If Mrs. Hayne's words sound a bit reverential, it's because the beard was, and still is, a Guinness-certified World Record, all 17 feet 6 inches of it.

Hans N. Langseth was born in Norway but lived most of his adult life in the Kensett area. Though it took him almost fifty years to grow his beard to such a prodigious length, little is known about why he grew it, how he kept it clean (it looks quite well-groomed in photographs), or how he avoided tripping on it when going about his business. In one photograph Hans is seated in an elaborately carved wooden chair with his beard hanging down his front past his knees and then curling up his right side, where the end lies draped over his shoulder. Did he pin the beard up on his shoulder every day? How did he hold his head up when he and his 17-foot beard got caught in a rainstorm? Did it bother his wife to have her husband's facial hair tickle her feet when they hugged? We don't know. Unfortunately, the man and his beard remain shrouded in mystery, and we're left with only questions—and almost 18 feet of facial hair tucked away in one of our national museums.

*Here rests Hans Langseth, but his beard rests in
the Smithsonian.*

Kensett, a tiny town with a post office, a library, a cafe, a bar, and not much else, doesn't have the beard and doesn't expect to be getting it back any time soon. At the close of her letter to Langseth's grandson, the Smithsonian's Mrs. Hayne said, "We will go through the routine steps of having the beard checked." An enigmatic statement leaving us with only more questions. What exactly are the routine steps for checking a beard? Does the Smithsonian really get so many beards sent to them that they have a beard-checking "routine"? And what sorts of things did they find when they checked Hans's beard? Brambles? A piece of dried fruitcake from 1912? A family of voles? In any case the beard checked out okay, was awarded the Guinness World Record, and now sits enshrined, the King of Beards, presumably in the Smithsonian's world-renowned Facial Hair Collection. You can't see the beard unless you head to D.C., but you can find photos of hirsute Hans at the Kensett historical museum, and you can visit Hans's grave, a large black-granite obelisk, at the Elk Horn cemetery a few miles west of Kensett. *NOTE*: Lest you married men get any ideas, Hans was a widower for more than thirty-five of his fifty years of beard growing. Coincidence? Probably not.

The Kensett Historical Museum is located in Kensett on U.S. Highway 65 in a deconsecrated church. Visits are by appointment only; call Sten Lucas at (641) 845–2304. To visit Hans Langseth's grave, travel west out of town on County Road A38 (Eighth Street) about 4 miles to Elk Creek Church. Langseth's grave is the tall black obelisk about halfway between A38 and the church. Be sure to check out the miniature version of Elk Creek Church right beside Elk Creek Church.

THE OLDEST LEMON CHIFFON IN IOWA
Marshalltown

Dating from 1887, Stone's restaurant is one of Iowa's oldest eateries and the only one owned and operated by fourth-generation restaurateurs, with a fifth-generation son running the kitchen. On any given night, Judy Stone might meet you at the glass-case candy counter just inside the front door and kindly show you past the original soda fountain to your table in the back. The Stone's most famous dish, their mile-high lemon chiffon pie, was first baked by Judy's mother-in-law's mother, Mrs. Anna Stone (be sure to put on your genealogical thinking cap if you start asking questions), which means diners have been topping off with these 6-inch-high slices of Midwestern decadence for more than seventy-five years. Clearly, long practice has made for perfect sinfulness: Epicurious Web site lists Stone's lemon chiffon as one of the top-10 pies in America.

The dark wood-paneled walls, ornate pressed-tin ceilings, and stools around the soda fountain counter all seem so authentically turn-of-the century because they in fact are turn-of-the-century. Just look at any of the old photographs lining the walls, and you'll see the restaurant appearing almost exactly the way it does now back in 1949 or in 1917 or in 1904, when it was just a cafe passenger stop on the railroad that still carries coal, corn oil, and freight past the Stone's doors. According to Judy the women in the family always ran the restaurant, even in 1887. So the only things that really change in the photographs on the wall are the decade and the Stone woman who happens to be in charge.

Stone's is located at 507 South Third Avenue in downtown Marshalltown. For more information call (641) 753–3626. The restaurant is open daily for lunch, dinner, and a special Sunday buffet from 11:00 A.M. to 3:00 P.M. Entrees include such faraway delicacies as shrimp and Alaskan King Crab legs. And be sure to save room for some of Grandma Anna Stone's pie. Or is it Great-grandma Anna Stone's pie?

A TREE HOUSE ON STEROIDS
Marshalltown

Sometime in the early 1980s, then college junior Michael Jurgensen asked his grandparents if he could build a deck on the back of their home, 3 miles east of Marshalltown. Parents and grandparents take note: Michael's grandparents said no, so he decided to build a simple platform in the silver maple out back instead. Twenty-one summers and a whole lot of lumber and man-hours later, the tree house is now a twelve-level, 55-foot-tall, 5,000-square-foot behemoth, with a microwave, refrigerator, lights, phone, running water, and a pretty darn good sound system to boot. The Jurgensen house still doesn't have a deck.

Michael, or Mick as his friends call him, showed an interest in all things mechanical from an early age. For his fifth birthday he asked his grandparents for 500 feet of speaker wire for a little home-sound-system project. Now in his early forties and a local elementary-school principal and music teacher, Mick still has a lot of enthusiasm for his experiment in arboreal architecture. "I've never had a plan for it," he said. "I just get excited about doing something new and wait for the next idea to come. When I start sketching and actually see it on paper, I know it's going to happen." And Mick has done an awful lot of sketching over the years. Just last summer he added an impressive five-story, sixty-step spiral staircase on the north end of the tree house. And more additions and improvements are surely brewing.

The tree house has grown so big that it's evolved into a wooden superstructure interlaced between the tree's large branches and dense foliage. There are rails and staircases between all levels except the eleventh and twelfth (you need to climb a ladder to get to the very top), but the whole structure is open, and with fourteen porch swings as well as numerous benches and picnic tables, there are lots of spots to sit and enjoy the great views. There are so many nooks and crannies, that it seems you could spend the whole day exploring the shady decks Mick's spent the last two decades building.

The Big Tree House is located at the Jurgensen's Shady Oaks Campground, which, when it opened in 1925, was the first cabin camp west of the Mississippi on the Lincoln Highway. Shaded by a grove of 200-year-old burr oaks, the campground is a beautiful spot to enjoy the ninety-seven channels on your RV's satellite TV. And should reruns get you down, you can retire to the Big Tree House, sit on a porch swing, and contemplate the questionable wisdom of saying "no deck" to an ambitious youngster.

To get to Shady Oaks Campground and the Big Tree House, take U.S. Highway 30 west out of Marshalltown for 3 miles. Take a left onto Shady Oaks Road and the tree house will be a quarter mile down the road on the left. Though the tree house is Mick's labor of love, his grandmother Mary Gift serves as tour guide, and visits are by appointment only. For more information or to make an appointment, call (641) 752–2946.

MARIONETTES IN THE MUSEUM
Mason City

*B*il Baird, world-famous twentieth-century puppet master whose credits include *Life with Snarky Parker,* the 1950 CBS-TV series, and *Winnie the Pooh* (1960), just happened to grow up in Mason City and graduate from Mason City High. You won't find reruns of his many successful movies and shows, not even on late-night cable, but if you want to see two gallery rooms full of his playful creations—the largest holding of his work to be found anywhere—you can visit the Charles H. Macnider Museum in downtown Mason City.

Housed in a 1920 Tudor-style building that was originally a private residence, the Macnider collection features many fine paintings, prints, photographs, and sculpture by American, Midwestern, and Iowa artists. Though the collection isn't nearly as large as that of a big-city museum, the quality of the work at the Macnider rivals that of any museum around, at least to this particularly unseasoned art critic. (The gallery of contemporary works is particularly impressive.)

But certainly the museum's most distinctive pieces are Baird's puppets, marionettes, and sketches, all housed in two adjoining rooms on the museum's second floor. The designs are fanciful, as marionettes should be, with weird distortions and disproportions: ears, eyes, and noses are cartoonishly large, hands look as if they've been inflated like balloons, cheeks are red as fire engines. There are lots of animal marionettes and puppets, of course, including a pelican, a crab, a lobster, a whole slew of *Winnie the Pooh* characters, and even a horse who seems to have found gainful employment as a belly dancer. Also included in the exhibit are some fascinating sketches Baird did in the planning stages of his puppet making, so you

Great art on display; lots of strings attached.

can get a look at his crafting process. Some big-city museum director might not consider Baird's marionettes fine art, but that's fine with the people at the Macnider, who honor an extremely talented hometown artist with lots of gallery space and attention, and it's more than fine with us.

In downtown Mason City directional signs near the intersection of U.S. Highways 18 and 65 lead visitors to the museum, which is located at 303 East Second Street. If you can't find the signs, take US 18 into Mason City, go north on Pennsylvania Avenue, and then take a right onto Second Street. The Macnider Museum will be on the right. Hours are 9:00 A.M. to 5:00 P.M. Wednesday, Fridays, and Saturdays, 9:00 A.M. to 9:00 P.M. on Tuesdays and Thursdays, and 1:00 to 5:00 P.M. on Sundays. For more information call (641) 421–3666.

BANK ROBBERS RUN
SHORT-LIVED TAXI SERVICE

*P*icture this scene: *A female employee in a room on the upper floor of a bank that is being robbed by armed men. She goes to a window and looks out onto a back alley, hoping to find someone, anyone who can help. Standing below her at the bank's back entrance is a short, thick-necked man dressed in a dark suit. "We're being robbed!" she shouts. "The bank is being robbed!" The man slowly turns and, looking up at her, brandishes a machine gun. In a calm, gruff voice he says, "You're telling me, lady?"*

Though it sounds like a scene from a Quentin Tarantino film, it really happened, right in downtown Mason City at the height of the Great Depression. The bank was the First National Bank, the man in the alley was Lester "Baby Face Nelson" Gillis, and the thug running the show inside was John Dillinger, the notorious gangster from Indiana. From September 1933 until July 1934, Dillinger and his gang terrorized the Midwest, robbing banks and police arsenals and staging three jail breaks (Dillinger himself broke out of jail using a fake wooden gun only ten days before the Mason City robbery), killing ten men and wounding seven others along the way.

On March 13, 1934, Dillinger, Baby Face Nelson, Homer Van Meter, Eddie Green, Tommy Carroll, and John Hamilton hit Mason City's First National Bank. The gang had hoped to net more than $240,000, a huge sum of money at the time, but due to a number of complications—not least of which was the fact that a bold teller named Harry Fisher kept passing Hamilton stacks of $1.00 bills instead of the larger denominations he demanded—they made off with only about $52,000. Dillinger's hopes to use his share of the big payoff to leave the country were dashed. He was shot and killed by FBI agents a little more than four months later, on July 22, outside the Biograph Theater in Chicago.

*A bank that wasn't such
an easy target.*

No one was
killed in the robbery,
but both Dillinger
and Hamilton
received shoulder
wounds, and one
bystander was shot
and wounded, by
either Hamilton or Baby Face Nelson, depending on the
account you happen to read. What is certain is that to make
their getaway, the gangsters used Mason City citizens as
human shields. According to reports they gathered hostages
from the bank to ride the running boards of their Packard
as they fled. Anne Youngdale recalled that Dillinger took
three of her mother's bridge-playing "lady friends" for a ride
far out into the countryside. "He put them all tied up on the
running boards so he wouldn't be shot," she said. "What a
ride! The ladies were released way out in nowhere." Reportedly, as the group passed slowly through town (the car could
go only 15 miles per hour because of all the weight), an
elderly hostage named Miss Minnie Piehm called out, "Let
me out! This is where I live!" And Dillinger let her off. Next
stop, nowhere!

The First National Bank is located in downtown Mason
City at the corner of State and Federal Streets.

A DEER IN NEED OF SUNSCREEN AND
SOME GOOD CAMO
St. Ansgar

Albino animals tend not to survive long because they have no camouflage, no way to hide from predators," says Guy Zenner of the Iowa Department of Natural Resources. "From a biological perspective it's a defect." Try telling that to the folks up in St. Ansgar, though, and you'll make some enemies mighty quick. During the 1980s an all-white deer living a few miles outside of town became the town's de facto mascot and most famous citizen. Not only did they lobby the Iowa legislature to prohibit the taking of predominantly white, white-tailed deer, they also stuffed and enshrined their own albino doe (after she died of natural causes, of course) in a cedar, glass-enclosed gazebo in the center of town.

St. Ansgar's albino deer was born in the spring of 1980 and, though biologically at risk, lived for eight and a half years within a 4-mile radius of where she was born. According to the plaque at her hooves, she gave birth to fifteen fawns, all normal color, and died in the winter of 1988 of pneumonia, kidney failure, and old age. (She also complained of aching joints, some memory and hearing loss, and constipation, in spite of all the good roughage in her diet.) Over the course of her long life, she became a town celebrity. The newspaper periodically wrote updates about her doings, families made trips to the fields at dusk to see if they could catch a glimpse of her feeding with her fawns, and a group of St. Ansgar citizens were instrumental in getting the Iowa legislature to help protect albino white-tailed deer from hunters.

And, of course, after she died town residents chipped in for a full-body mount and displayed her first at the Heartland

Power Cooperative and then downtown in a small park right across from Village Hardware. She stands—head tilted slightly to the left, pink eyes gazing at the building across the street—in a rectangular glass case inside a glass-enclosed cedar gazebo with a little cupola on top. Inside there's a plaque giving the bare facts of her life, some fake snow and dried cornhusks on the floor to give the scene a wintry look, framed documents signed by Governor Bransted having something to do with the albino-deer-protection legislation, and two 8-by-12-inch photographs of the deer standing in winter fields, corn stubble at her feet.

It's no accident St. Ansgar chose flattering winter scenes to display their beloved albino deer. In spring, summer, and fall, a white coat might not be the best camouflage, but it's certainly no liability during the long northern Iowa winters.

St. Ansgar's albino deer is right downtown across from Village Hardware at the corner of Fourth and Mitchell.

CANDY BARS WELL PAST THEIR EXPIRATION DATES
State Center

Small-town general stores aren't a dying breed; they're officially extinct, gone the way of the house-call-making doctor, the milkman, and, for a more classic example, the dodo bird. The reasons are by now as familiar as they seem inevitable: small communities losing population (and young people in particular) to urban areas, a struggling farm economy, big box stores, with their huge volume discounts, cropping up at every busy intersection in America.

Want a positive side bar to this extinction tale? Well, imagine a community loving their tiny grocery store so much that

Vintage clothing yes, vintage groceries no.

the whole town pitched in to preserve it. Located in downtown State Center, Watson's Grocery was built in 1885 and managed to serve the community for almost one hundred years until then-owner Ralph Watson died in 1979. The place was boarded up for the next decade until his widow died and the heirs decided to put it up for auction. When locals got wind of the plan to sell, they formed a citizens group, raised funds any way they could, went to the auction, and emerged the highest bidders. Finally, they set about renovating and cleaning up the store—a lot of dust can pile up on the canned corn in ten years—and turned it into an authentic small-town grocery museum.

Inside you'll find the store's original oak cabinetry, an old-fashioned register, and lots and lots of period grocery items and dry goods, including canned vegetables, candy bars, sacks of flour and salt, and various old-fashioned sundries. Some of the trade names are familiar—you can choose between Milky Ways and Mounds in the candy section, for example—but you'll also find unfamiliar items, like Dr. I.Q., a candy bar presumably made either by or for smart people. And all the packaging is unfamiliar, giving you a delicious feeling of having stepped back in time to a different era, when the grocer knew your name (and even your dog's name) and you bought your flour and soap on credit. Just don't get too excited to try the Dr. I.Q.s if you visit; even if there were some left in the box, they'd be about sixty or seventy years past their expiration dates.

Watson's Grocery is located at 106 West Main Street in downtown State Center. It's open 1:00 to 4:00 P.M. Friday through Sunday. For more information or to schedule a visit, call (515) 483–2458 or (515) 483–2110.

IOWA'S NINETEENTH-, TWENTIETH-, AND TWENTY-FIRST-CENTURY INDIAN ENTREPRENEURS
Tama

After the Black Hawk War of 1832, a sort of last stand for Native Americans along the Mississippi, a series of Indian land cessions in Iowa between 1832 and 1845 left tribes like the Mesquaki (also known as the Fox tribe) without any land at all. The government forced the removal of the Mesquaki to a reservation in northeastern Kansas in 1845, and of the 1,227 tribe members who made the journey from east-central Iowa, fewer than half survived due to an epidemic of smallpox.

Sounds like a familiar tale, no? But wait, the story actually takes a turn for the better. Around 300 Mesquaki Indians remained behind, refusing to leave; within a few years, other tribe members returned from Kansas, and the group lived quietly along the banks of the Iowa River for ten years before the state passed a law "allowing" the Mesquaki to stay. (I don't think they were planning on going anywhere.) Then, on July 13, 1857, the Iowa Mesquaki purchased their first eighty acres in Tama County along the banks of the Iowa. (The only reason the seller did business with the Mesquaki was greed: They were willing to pay $1,000 for the parcel, nearly ten times what a white man had to pay.) The Mesquaki once again had a homeland.

And the homelands grew. Each year between 1857 and 1866, the tribe purchased more acreage by trading trees, horses, and furs. In 1867, the United States finally began paying the tribe annuities for the land it had stolen, excuse us, "bought," back in the 1830s for about 10 cents an acre, and the Indian land purchases grew in size. By 1901 the Mesquaki had

An old photo of a Mesquaki tribe member in traditional dress.
Photo: Catherine Cole

amassed 3,000 acres, and by 1987, the tribe owned outright a total of 7,054 acres of land in the center of the state of Iowa.

With a tribal enrollment of 1,163 people, the Mesquaki community is now a vital part of the economic and cultural life in Tama County. They opened a 127,669-square-foot casino, with four restaurants and an attached 208-room hotel, which employs more than 1,000 people. (Currently the tribe is involved in a divisive battle over two separate leadership councils, a battle that has shut down the casino, but officials hope the matter will be resolved soon.) And each August, on the original eighty-acre parcel it bought almost 150 years ago, the tribe holds the Mesquaki Powwow, a four-day-long event based historically on a ceremony called the Green Corn Dance, during which the community came together to visit, rest, and celebrate the harvest. Persons outside the community are welcome to attend the ceremonial dances along the Iowa River. According to tribe historian Jonathan Buffalo, though, inviting those outside the tribe has been a rather recent development. And with a history like theirs, who can blame the Mesquaki for being a little cautious about inviting the neighbors.

The Mesquaki casino and settlement are located just south of Tama off U.S. Highway 63. The casino is at 1504 305th Street. For general information call (515) 484–2108; for more information about the Mesquaki Powwow, held each year in mid-August, call (515) 484–4678 or (515) 484–5358.

S I L O   P E N T H O U S E   w / V I E W
T i t o n k a

You've probably heard of barns being converted into designer, exposed-beam homes, but what about moving the whole family into the silo out back? Just think of all that great space wasted on feed. And think of all the things a Midwestern Martha Stewart could do with a 40-foot-tall metal cylinder, a charge card, and a little imagination.

If you want an example of how to turn a silo into a home, complete with penthouse on top, then you need look no farther than northern Iowa. Arthur "Hap" Peterson built his silo home—the only one in the state, as far as we can tell—back in 1983. He bought a new Madison silo for the project, fitted it with specially constructed metal frames for the windows, and then built four floors inside. The ground level features a laundry, half-bath, and office; the second floor a family and entertainment room; the third floor a bedroom and full bath; and the fourth the kitchen and dining rooms. To top it all off, Hap built a wooden penthouse on the ground, with six picture windows and a true wraparound porch, and then raised the structure to the top of the silo by crane. The end architectural effect is truly notable, a cross between giant agricultural scepter and Midwestern lighthouse.

Titonka is on County Road P66 north of US 18. Silo Home tours are by appointment only. Call Arthur Peterson at (515) 928–2734.

A BUTTER SCULPTURE IN BRONZE
Toledo

Duffy knows cows: Jersey, Guernsey, Holstein, Milking Shorthorn, Ayrshire, Brown Swiss. You name your favorite Iowa ruminant, and she knows it by heart (and by hand). Not only is Norma "Duffy" Lyons a dairy farmer with a 1,300-acre operation in Toledo, she also happens to be the woman who's sculpted the Iowa State Fair's butter cow each year since 1960. "I can sculpt any dairy breed you can think of off the top of my head," she says matter-of-factly. And for proof, you need look no farther than her life-sized butter cows. If they weren't colored a low-moisture, pure-cream-Iowa-butter yellow, you'd think they were entries in the livestock show.

The seventy-four-year-old Lyons achieves these remarkable results with some rather messy materials and less than pleasant working conditions. She starts by softening about 600 pounds of frozen butter at room temperature, most of which is recycled from last year's butter cow. (They started recycling after the sponsors griped about how pricey butter was by the half ton.) Once the butter thaws enough to be worked, she begins applying it to a wood-and-wire-mesh frame she built into the vague shape of a cow. Duffy begins on the head and neck, works her way down the body, and then ends with the legs and hooves. Oh, and did we mention the whole sculpting process takes place in a 42-degree (F) cooler? Each August for the past forty-three years, Duffy has put on her jacket and ear-muffs, stepped into the cooler in the fairground's Agriculture Building, shoved her hand into a five-gallon bucket of butter, taken out a hunk, and worked her magic.

But Duffy doesn't know just cows. She's also done some impressive butter sculptures of other subjects, and part of the anticipation surrounding each state fair is the question of what Duffy is going to sculpt next. In summers past she's made creamy versions of everyone from Charlie Brown to Elvis, to Garth Brooks, and to Jesus and his apostles, all of which have drawn fair-goers by the thousands. People frequently stand in line just to get a look at her creations. And this past summer, she sculpted a beautiful life-sized Harley Davidson, a butter hawg that looked strangely at home beside Duffy's tried-and-true butter cow.

Duffy's talents have brought her quite a bit of work, and quite a bit of attention, over the years. Toledo commissioned a bronze cow and calf for display in town, and her sculptures have been displayed at county and state fairs in thirteen states and in Canada. She's been the subject of countless radio, news-paper, and magazine stories (both local and national), and she appeared on the *Today Show* and *Late Night with David Letter-man*. Maybe it's the firm-footed farmer in her, but Duffy doesn't seem too impressed by any of it. "I've been on the Letterman show. He flew me out to New York, bought one seat for me and one for a cow I molded out of cheese. It was O.K., I guess." It's pretty tough to impress Duffy Lyons, but somehow impressing Iowans year after year is second nature to her.

Duffy's bronze cow and calf is located at the northwest junc-tion of U.S. Highways 63 and 30 in Toledo. For information call

(641) 484–4193. The Iowa State Fair is held each August at the Iowa State Fair Grounds just off I–80 in Des Moines. Take I–80 to exit 141 (US 65), and then take US 65 south to exit 79. Follow University Avenue west to the fairgrounds. For more information about the fair, call (800) 545–3247 or visit www.iowa statefair.org.

MORE SHAKERS THAN YOU CAN SHAKE A STICK AT
Traer

R uth Rasmussen may seem like a typical Iowa grandmother. She's got white hair, she knits, and she's just about the most hospitable and welcoming woman you'll ever meet. But she also has the Guinness-record-book-certified largest collection of salt and pepper shakers in the world, as well as enough dogged determination and independence to remind you this was once a land of pioneers. If collecting 14,000 of anything isn't proof enough of iron will, just listen to Mrs. Rasmussen speak. She's fond of saying, "I don't care," with a devilish twinkle in her eye, as in, I don't care what people think. "People tell me I should sell them and take the money. But I don't care; I want to keep them." She'll say it again when you notice her recumbent (and headless) nude-woman shakers, with the salt in one detachable breast and pepper in the other. "People say, 'Oh, what are you doing with that one,' but I don't care." Oh, and did we mention she's seventy-nine and still works, taking care of, as she says, "old people"?

There's a small sign in front of her house a few blocks east of town on Highway 8. If you stop and ring the bell, she'll take you around back and show you two big sheds full of every kind of shaker you can imagine (and thousands you couldn't have

The easiest grandmother in the world to shop
for—another salt and pepper shaker set it is!
Photo: Catherine Cole

imagined): She's got Empire State buildings; sumo wrestlers;
ballerinas; cartoon characters; every kind of wild and domesti-
cated animal, from cows to lions to very, very long dogs; commemorative shakers from Princess Di's wedding; all fifty
states; and corn, corn, and more corn (this is Iowa after all).
She's also got all the U.S. Presidents, except for the current
Bush—no prejudice there, she just hasn't gotten around to cut-
ting out his portrait and pasting it onto a plain white shaker,
as she had to do with the elder Bush and Clinton, since the
company that made presidential shakers went out of business.

If you're interested, she'll take you inside, introduce you to her husband, Cecil (who bought her a beautiful pair of tiny crystal shakers for their 50th wedding anniversary and, dear saint, helps her dust them all), and show you the rest of her collection. The highlight just might be a shaker with Bill and Hillary's heads bobbing back and forth atop the White House: Hillary shakes her head no, whereas Bill shakes his head yes. Who would have guessed there are shakers that deliver presidential political analysis as well as salt and pepper?

The World's Largest Salt and Pepper Shaker Collection is located on Highway 8, a few blocks east of town. Look for the small real estate–style sign that says, WORLD'S LARGEST SALT AND PEPPER SHAKER COLLECTION—COME ON IN!

NEED AN EXOTIC CHICK?
Webster City

Take out a pencil, put your books on the floor, and move your desk away from your neighbor's—we're having a pop chicken quiz. Yes, answers need to be in complete sentences. And we won't start until the young man in the back stops making the clucking noises.

- How can you tell if a hen will lay brown eggs or white eggs?
- Is it possible to tell whether an egg is fresh without cracking it open? If so, how does one go about determining an egg's freshness?
- Extra credit: What's the world's largest mail-order chick hatchery?

The answer to the extra-credit question is Murray McMurray Chicks, a rare-breed hatchery and mail-order chick company in

Is that peeping I hear coming from the mailbox?

Webster City, and the first two questions came directly from the list of frequently asked questions on McMurray's Web site (see answers below). Murray McMurray started his chicken business back in 1917. He was in banking at the time, but he sold baby chicks through the bank to area farmers up until the early stages of the depression, when his bank went bust. Then he decided to go into the hatchery and mail-order chick business full time. And the rest, as they say in Webster City, is history.

For years McMurray Chicks was run out of a private residence at 609 Ohio Street, which had been converted to a hatchery, but not long ago they built a 24,000-square-foot facility that can hatch up to 100,000 chicks a week. Rare-breed varieties for sale include Buff Brahmas, with their dramatically feathered feet; White Crested Black Polish, featuring large white crests that resemble old-fashioned judges' wigs; Turkens, which have completely bare turkeylike necks; and Red Frizzle Cochins, with feathers that curve outward and forward, giving them the appearance of having just walked 5 miles backward into a stiff wind. Most chicks sell for around $3.00 apiece, but you need to order at least a dozen. McMurray ships them express and guarantees 100 percent live arrival at your door. (But since travel time can take two or three days, be prepared to receive some hungry, and noisy, chicks on your doorstep.)

Answers: So how can you tell if a hen will lay brown eggs or white, class? Check their earlobes. (What, you didn't know chickens had earlobes? And you call yourself a Midwesterner.) Chickens with red earlobes will lay brown eggs, whereas chickens with white earlobes will lay white ones. And how do you tell if an egg that you found in the henhouse after a week's vacation is fresh? Easy. Just set it in water. Fresh eggs haven't had time to absorb much air, so they sink; eggs that aren't so fresh float.

For homework study the Murray McMurray Web site at www.mcmurrayhatchery.com. Tours aren't offered. Class dismissed.

INDEX

ABOUT THE AUTHORS

Dan Coffey is best known as public radio's Dr. Science. He was a cofounder of the comedy troupe called Duck's Breath Mystery Theater, which performed for twelve years in San Francisco. Coffey and fellow comedian, Merle Kessler, developed the *Ask Dr. Science* show, which has been a staple on public radio since 1983. Coffey now makes his home in Iowa City, Iowa, where he continues to write in a humorous vein.

Eric Jones is an east coast transplant, having come to Iowa City to attend the University of Iowa's Nonfiction Writing Program. He writes about health, medicine, and travel, and currently works as a household mover and as a nursing assistant at the University of Iowa's Burn Treatment Center. This is his first book.

Contributor Berit Thorkelson, a travel writer currently living in Des Moines, Iowa, is no longer obsessed with the World's Largest Cheeto. She's merely fond of it. Her stories about destinations in the Midwest and worldwide have appeared in magazines and newspaper travel sections, including the *Minneapolis–St. Paul Star Tribune*, the *Chicago Tribune*, and *Midwest Living* magazine.

THE INSIDER'S SOURCE

With more than 120 Midwest-related titles, we have the area covered. Whether you're looking for the path less traveled, a favorite place to eat, family-friendly fun, a breathtaking hike, or enchanting local attractions, our pages are filled with ideas to get you from one state to the next.

For a complete listing of all our titles, please visit our Web site at www.GlobePequot.com. The Globe Pequot Press is the largest publisher of local travel books in the United States and is a leading source for outdoor recreation guides.

FOR BOOKS TO THE MIDWEST